𝒜nd
  You
  Shall
  Teach
  Them
  Diligently
  To
  Your
  Children…

And You Shall Teach Them Diligently To Your Children...

Transmitting Jewish Values From Generation To Generation

By
STEVEN BAYAR *with* Naomi Eisenberger
Edited by Leora Wiener

TOWN HOUSE PRESS
Somers, New York

Copyright © 2010 by Steven Bayar
All rights reserved.

Library of Congress Catalogue Number 2010929395
International Standard Book Number: 0-940653-52-4

Printed in the United States of America

Published by
The Town House Press
438E Heritage Hills, Somers, New York 10589

For additional information:
Steven Bayar, Rabbi
43 Haran Circle
Millburn, New Jersey 07041

And You Shall Teach Them Diligently to Your Children...

Dedication

To My Parents:
Max z'l* and Blanche Bayar z'l
For what they gave me.

To My Family:
Leora, Rahel, Tuvi, Meira and Merav
For teaching me how to give

To My Granddaughter:
Ma'ayan
For showing me my children's values

Dedication

To
ANNIE z'l AND MORRIS NEGRIN z'l
*Grandparents who first showed me that a simple life of
doing good for others could bring joy and inner peace.*

To
MOLLY z'l AND GEORGE KAPLAN z'l
*Who continued down that same road, modeling goodness
and service to others in all that they did.*

To
GERRY, ANDREW, SARA, JENNIE AND MICHAEL
*The way you lead your lives, with concern for and
attention to others less fortunate, has proven that
our family's lessons have been well-instilled.*

And finally, to those "jewels" that every parent dreams about:
MEITAL, ILAN, MOLLIE, ALEXANDRA AND DAFNA
*I hope that the lessons this family has taught for generations
about a life of doing for others will carry on as you
grow to maturity.*

*Zichronum Liv'racha – May their names be a blessing

The Good People everywhere
Will teach anyone who wants to know
How to fix all things breaking and broken in
This world --
Including hearts and dreams --
And along the way we will learn such things as
Why we are here
And what we are supposed to be doing
With our hands and minds and souls and our time.
That way, we can hope to find out why
We were given a human heart
And that way, we can hope to know
The hearts of other human beings
And the heart of the world.

By Danny Siegel

Table of Contents

Tips For Reading This Book. 6

Author's Introduction. 7

Section I. Foundations: Introduction. 9

1. Who, What And How Do You Want Your Children To Be?. . . .10
   Community Voices: Meira Bayar
   Tuna Subs & Air Conditioners

2. Why? Combating The "Tevye Syndrome.". 15

3. What Are Your Values, And Do You Share Them With Your Children?. 20
   Community Voices: Sharon Halper
   The (*Not So*) Secret World Of Grandparents:
   One GrandFamily's *Tikun Olam* Tale

4. The Vocabulary Of The Jewish Community. 26

Section II: Mitzvot: Introduction 34

5. *How The Supermarket Aisles Can Teach Kids About Hunger*
   Feeding The Hungry – *Lechem L'Re'eyvim*. 35
   Good Person: Clara Hammer z'l

6. *Caring For Elders Is Not A Visit With Grandma*
   Respect For The Elderly – *Lehader Pnai Zaken*. 39
   Good Person: Dr. William Thomas

7. *Sticks & Stones: Names Hurt More*
   Do Not Use Evil Language – *Lashon Harah*. 44
   Good Person: Neto Villereal

8. *A Lesson In Humility*
   Visiting People Who Are Ill – *Bikur Cholim*. 49
   Good People: Mike & Sue Turk

Community Voices: Andrea Hirschfeld
  Mitzvah Clowning, And Your Child's Self Esteem

9. *To Care For Others **Is** To See The Face Of God*
  Hospitality – *Hachnesat Orchim*. 57
  Good Person: Yoel Dorkam

10. *Compassion Does Not End When Life Does*
  Respect For That Which Has Lived – *K'vod Hamet*. 62
  Good Person: Jeannie Jaybush

11. *Murder In A Different Form?*
  Do Not Waste – *Bal Tashchit*. 67
  Good Person: Ranya Kelly

12. *The Earth Is Ours And The Glory Thereof*
  Guarding The Earth/Ecology – *Shomrei Adamah*. 72
  Good Person: Andy Lipkis

13. *We **Are** Our Brother's Keeper*
  Do Not Stand Idly By – *Al Ta'amod*. 78
  Good Person: Jay Feinberg

14. *Half a World Away Is Still Next Door*
  Redeeming The Captive - *Pidyon Shevuyim*. 82
  Good People: Broad Meadows Kids

15. *Everyone Counts, Everyone*
  Respect For All Human Life – *Meshaneh Habriyot*. 88
  Good Person: Hadassah Levi
  Community Voices: Nina B. Mogilnik
    Integration Is A Two-Way Street
  Community Voices: Beth Horowitz Giladi
    A Successful Community Beats With One Heart

  Section III. Introduction to Tzedakah 108

16. *The Dynamics Of Giving*. 110
  Good Person: Dr. Eliezer Jaffe

17. *The First Step*...................................120
      Community Voices: Diane Lipszyc
         Involving Your Children In *Tzedakah* Decisions

18. *The Laws Of Tzedakah*............................125

19. *Maimonides Eight Degrees Of* Tzedakah...........130

20. *Fraud*...134

Section IV. The Holy Days, Chagim 139

21. *What Is "Holy" About A Holiday?*................139

22. *Rosh Hashanah & Yom Kippur, Yamim Nora'im*......140

23. *Sukkot*..145

24. *Chanukah*..148

25. *Purim*...152

26. *Pesach*..155

    Shavuot..158

28. *Shabbat*...162

29. *In Conclusion*...................................165

Section V. Appendices 167

I. Maimonides Description Of *Lashon Harah* – Evil Language..167

II. Bill Emerson Good Samaritan Food Law.............168

III. Annotated Bibliography...........................172

IV. Annotated Videography............................175

This book is intended for the family. There is something in here for everyone: children, parents and grandparents.

Tips For Reading This Book

1. If you are reading this book as a family, you might have the youngest pick out the parts to be read – their attention is our priority.

2. If you only plan to flip through the book, read the "Good People" profiles at the beginning of the chapters and the stories at the end. You will find them the most interesting for the time allowed.

3. This book is not sequential; you can read it out of order. Each chapter stands alone. Find an interesting topic and enjoy.

4. If you are looking for quick activities for the family, read the "Home Work" sections first.

Should you have a question about anything in this book – contact the author. I welcome the interaction.

Author's Introduction

I was introduced to the values I hold most dear by my parents. These values provided the foundation that has helped stabilize me through life. They have been whetted, honed and distilled through my life experiences in the various congregations I have held, people I have met and experiences I have encountered.

My parents passed away years ago. Yet they still live with me every day. Ironically, the older I get the more I understand them. Their actions and attitudes that seemed alien to me when I was younger make perfect sense today. Ironically, though lost to me now, I have never been closer to them. And so I find myself this morning walking to our synagogue's summer camp with my two year old granddaughter. After I drop her off I have to call Naomi Eisenberger, director of the GOOD PEOPLE FUND to firm up plans for our upcoming trip to Myra and McRoberts, Kentucky – two towns in the poorest section of Appalachia (the poorest section of the United States. Our congregation will be traveling there soon to bring trucks of food and clothing to support the poor people in those communities.

As I walk with my granddaughter hand in little hand, my parents are at my side. I see the patterns of our lives intertwined but how can I faithfully transmit what I have been given and insure that I teach her as well?

Being part of her life as she grows and matures is part of the answer. Giving her the opportunity to visit places like McRoberts is another. This book is the third part. We teach our children (and grandchildren) by *being* the lessons we seek to teach. It is not enough to facilitate the experiences; we must own them as well.

The key element we need to make this happen is the story. As I will note further on, we are a community that tells and lives stories. Stories can instruct and illustrate. This is a book where stories, stories of people, present and past, have combined to teach us about the values that are the foundation of our tradition.

I am blessed to have a family that is an abiding source of support in my life, my Congregation Bnai Israel in Millburn, New Jersey has challenged me to work and grow (not always voluntarily) in ways I could never envision, my students both child and adult who have encouraged me to learn and grow in a variety of directions and my friends who have stayed with me through it all.

I am privileged to belong to a profession where doing *Mitzvah* work is part of the job description – and a congregation where *Tikun Olam* has become an expected part of congregational life. All these influences have created for me a "perfect storm" that was the inspiration for this book.

One further note. It is true that "by giving we receive." At the darkest times of my life, I have learned to (eventually) pick myself up off the couch and force myself to leave the house because I had Mitzvah responsibilities. I have learned over the years that the best cure for the darkness is helping others.

My special thanks go to Naomi Eisenberger for challenging me and working with me in this endeavor, for having the intestinal fortitude to establish the Good People Fund and for her skillful editing of this book. In my "book" we are a team.

Blessed are You, Lord our God, Sovereign of the universe, who has kept us alive, sustained us and allowed us to reach this day.

Section One: Foundations: Introduction

In 1998 the Righteous Persons Foundation awarded a grant to the Giraffe Project and the *Ziv Tzedakah* Fund to publish a curriculum on *Tzedakah*. The curriculum found its way into over 800 institutions throughout the world. This book is an extension of the curriculum. The curriculum was intended for both formal and informal educational settings; classroom, youth group and camps. This book is intended for intergenerational use; parents, grandparents and children.

I once gave a workshop at the Chicago Board of Jewish Education in which a prominent educator from a major congregation made the following observation, "From the moment a student walks into our building they see *Tzedakah* at work; boxes for food drives, clothing drives, infant furniture drives, it's all there. We are always collecting for something. So why don't our students care about *Tzedakah*?" I suggested to him that the students perceived the drives as manifestations of adult values, not something they needed to be a part of. They had no reason to participate.

This first part of the book provides the philosophical foundation for *Tzedakah* and *Tzedakah*-related activities (*Mitzvot*). As noted below, we too often perform the actions without understanding why. If we are to effectively pass on values from one generation to another we must be able to teach the *why* as well as the *how.*

We are the people of the Covenant. Our Covenant with God gives us a unique perspective in that we have both expectations of, and responsibilities to God. This dynamic allows us to create a Covenant community and provides for support and continuity.

Chapter 1: Who, What And How Do You Want Your Children To Be?

A Parent who denies a child religious knowledge robs him of his inheritance. (Sanhedrin 1b)

There is so much more to life than a perfectly clean kitchen floor. (Rachel Naomi Remen)

As a rabbi I get many questions about both my professional and personal life. One of the most interesting questions I am asked is "what type of children do I want to raise?" Do I want them to go to a good college (if affordable, yes)? Do I want them to be well off? (nice, but not necessary). Do I want them Jewish? (definitely, yes) What do I want most for them? The answer to that is contained in this story:

In the days when an ice cream sundae cost much less, a ten year old boy entered a hotel coffee shop and sat at a table. A waitress put a glass of water in front of him and waited for his order.
"How much is an ice cream sundae?"
"Fifty cents," replied the waitress.
The little boy pulled his hand out of his pocket and studied a number of coins in it.
"How much is a dish of plain ice cream?"
Some people were now waiting for a table and the waitress was a bit impatient.
"Thirty five cents," she said, a little brusquely.
The little boy again counted the coins and said, "I'll have the plain ice cream."
The waitress brought the ice cream, put the bill on the table and walked away. The boy finished his ice cream, paid the cashier and departed. When the waitress came back, she picked up the empty plate and then swallowed hard at what she saw. There, placed neatly beside the empty dish, were two nickels and five pennies, fifteen cents, the difference between a scoop and a sundae – her tip.

I want them to be compassionate enough to think a person, overworked and not very likable, is still more important than fudge and whipped cream.

Each of us is the main character in the story of our lives. We share ourselves with others by telling our stories and it is through stories that we often learn the greatest lessons. We live within the framework of stories about success and failure or good and evil. Our self perception is seen through these narratives.

There is a reason that the *Torah* begins with stories. The entire book of Genesis and the first half of the book of Exodus tells the story of our people. These stories have a power that transcends time and history. Our history changed at Sinai. With revelation came law. The law forms the foundation of our religious practice and belief but it does not speak to our aspirations and yearnings. We need law and observance for continuity. However we need our stories for our souls.

This is a book for families. The family is the foundational building block of our religion. The primary values of our tradition are woven into the fabric of the family dynamic. We learn this from the logic sequence of the *Shma,* "Hear Israel, the Lord is our God, the Lord alone…You shall love your God with all your soul…You shall teach this diligently to your children." The responsibility of teaching the concept of loving God is given to the parents. Our tradition teaches that we show our love of God by performing *Mitzvot*.

This is a book of stories; stories tied to the law that help us understand and apply the law. These stories form the narrative of your personal Jewish history and it is hoped will become the cornerstone of your Jewish identity.

People come to me seeking help. They are often sad, depressed and desperate. They want to stop hurting. They want to keep their demons at bay. They want to find fulfillment. Invariably I tell them that there are no short-term cures. Sometimes it takes "as long as you have had the pain" to resolve it. But I can prescribe something for the short term, something that will take away the fear and the frustration and keep you sane while you get the long-term help. It is called "helping others." Find an organization that provides immediate care for the poor, the sick or the homeless. I tell them to find someone who needs you and feed them, clothe them or help them out of their misery. I have tried this. It works.

How do we create caring children? We must start with ourselves: People ask me what kind of person I aspire to be. I say to them, "Let me tell you a true story," for stories are sometimes more effective than advice. To properly understand I must share with you something that others who know me would never believe; I am painfully shy. I have a hard time talking to people I don't know. Needless to say, in my work as a Rabbi I have had to overcome this shyness. However, I still have a hard time in purely social situations. I would have failed the following quiz simply because I would be too shy to ask.

During my second month of nursing school, our professor gave us a pop quiz. I was a conscientious student and had breezed through the questions, until I read the last one:

"What is the first name of the woman who cleans the school?"

Surely this was some kind of joke. I had seen the cleaning woman several times. She was tall, dark haired and in her 50's. But how would I know her name? I handed in my paper, leaving the question blank. Before class ended, one student asked if the last question would count toward our quiz grade.

"Absolutely" said the professor. "In your careers you will meet many people. All are significant. They deserve your attention and care, even if all you do is smile and say hello."

I've never forgotten that lesson. I also learned her name was Dorothy.

Bob Thobol (Giraffe Project)

Community Voices
Air Conditioners & Tuna Subs
by Meira Bayar[1]

Walking down the street on that the August day, I saw a homeless woman sitting outside a sandwich shop, something that is not out of place on the New York City streets. As I walked by, something made me stop and take a second glance. Unlike others, she wasn't asking for money, she was asking for food. As my friends crossed the street to avoid her, I stayed and offered, "You guys go on wyithout me, I'll meet up with you in a second". I went in to the shop and bought three tuna subs, milk and a few apples. On my way out I handed the food to the woman, wished her a good day and went to meet up with my friends.

Not all of my friends had gone on without me; Josh wanted to make sure I didn't get lost, so he watched me from across the street. He commented, "That was really nice of you, but it isn't really safe, and it's not like you can solve anything with a tuna sub." I didn't really know what to respond. The truth was I couldn't put into words why I had done it, just that I knew that I should.

Today, years later, I know why I did it. We all went to Jewish day school, and Jewish sleep away camp for years, yet those experiences never prepared me for that situation on that day. But two weeks before the "tuna sub incident," I had spent a hot summer Sunday afternoon in my Hebrew tutor's apartment. It was very hot in the apartment. My tutor didn't have an air conditioner –they had just had their first baby and air conditioners were expensive. They didn't have the money. When my father came to pick me up he said that, as coincidence had it, he knew someone in the community who had an extra air conditioner, and "was looking to get rid of it." With the connection made, my father

---

[1] Meira Bayar, MSW, recently graduated from Columbia University School of Social Work in New York City. Her focus is clinical work in the area of trauma. She received her BA from Rutgers University in Women's and Gender Studies, with a minor in Jewish Studies.

promised my tutor to drop it off later that day. In the car my father asked me, "Would you mind if we made one stop before we go home?" We drove straight to the closest hardware store. Inside, we picked out the best air conditioner they sold, ripped the price tag off, and dropped it at their apartment.

We never discussed the 'air conditioner incident' until years later, when reminiscing over a cup of coffee. I turned to him and remarked, "You know, I try so hard to be like you, let me tell you my own story about some tuna subs...."

Many times we assume that by *telling* our children what is right and wrong, they will learn. If we send them to the best schools, and make sure they have the most amazing summer experiences they will learn Jewish values; *chesed, Tzedakah, G'milut Chasadim,* (loving acts) and more. While that may be true, nothing can compare to the effect parents' actions have on their children.

Chapter 2: Why? Combating the "Tevye" Syndrome

If you have learned much Torah, do not hold fast to it for yourself, but teach it to others, for that is why you were created   (Avot 2:8)

The only thing necessary for the triumph of evil is for good men to do nothing.   (Edmund Burke)

Part of my Journey

In my last year of Seminary I traveled up and down the East Coast on job interviews. The interviews all felt the same; the same questions repeated by the same type of people. No matter the venue, "How are you with children?", "What would you say to a sick person?", "How do you like what you see?" and "What would you change?" were constant companions. Yet each congregation had its own story to tell; a story I desperately needed to hear. The stories were there but the committees did not always know how to communicate their tales to me.

I soon learned that the easiest way to learn what I needed to know was to accept the "interview argument" when it was offered. Each congregation has issues that divide it, especially when dealing with continuity; how will the new rabbi change what we are comfortable with? Consciously or not, each rabbinical candidate is "set up" with a tough issue with both sides represented on the committee. Every interview committee has at least one curmudgeon, placed there to be argumentative with the candidate. The curmudgeon offers an argument and everyone watches to see if the "fur will fly." The candidate is in no small measure evaluated by how they respond to the curmudgeon and how they handle the argument (not always which side they take). I knew the questions would surely come – I just had to wait.

As the issue would present itself and the committee would disintegrate into chaos, if instead of trying to make peace in the committee or take an immediate stand (as most candidates do) I would allow the argument to unfold – I would learn more about the dynamics of the congregation without hurting my chances at being hired.

And so, in one suburban Philadelphia congregation, the issue centered upon religious observances and values:

"Rabbi, what topics will you speak about from the *Bimah*?"

"*I speak about ethical issues, behavior and the portion of the week.*"

"Rabbi, aren't you going to talk about *Kashrut* (the dietary laws) and how important it is to keep *kosher*?"

"*I don't do that. People don't listen when you tell them what to do. I don't want to waste their time or mine. Why would you want me to talk about Kashrut?*"

"Because I want my children to know what is right and what is wrong."

"*Well, do you keep kosher?*"

"No."

"*Then you are asking me to tell your children not only to keep kosher, but that their father is doing something wrong.*"

Chaos ensued. After a lively discussion that I took no part in, I made the following statement:

"*I'll tell you what. I'm not going to talk about keeping kosher from the bimah. Instead, I will become friends with your children. They will become fixtures in my home. They will baby-sit for my family, eat with me and become very close. They will see me as a role model. Then, one day, under my influence, they will tell you that they want to keep kosher. They will tell you that they won't eat in your home unless the home is kosher. Then, what will you do?*"

"I will get you fired."

While I was later offered the pulpit, I refused. I found that I was changed by these interviews. I learned a new perspective of the rabbinate and the community. In many communities Jewish educators have adversarial relationships with parents.[2] From the educator's point of view, we find that the values and observances we teach our students often conflict with their home and secular lives. We resent that children are taken out of class early for baseball practice in the spring or that the family insists on going skiing on a given winter weekend. We feel

---

[2] How they can work together is the subject of many articles and discussions.

neglected when parents feel they know more about what their children need to know than we do. We are sad knowing that certain students attain great heights as *Bnai Mitzvah* only to have their parents remove them from things Jewish immediately after. The battle lines are drawn as parents and educators fight over what they think are the souls of their children.

From the parent's point of view, educators are not sensitive to the very real issues families face in our society. Jewish educators live in ivory towers, send their children to day schools and are usually more observant than the people they serve. Educators and parents do not speak the same language. When the two major issues in middle school (yes, middle school) are drinking and oral sex, Judaism is a distant third.

Many times parents and educators lack mutual respect. Both tend to be self centered. Educators tend to think that someone unversed in the Jewish tradition is simplistic and unsophisticated. Parents tend to view anyone who has voluntarily accepted the restrictive life and salary of Jewish education is not living up to their potential and can be easily manipulated.

The results? Educators burn out and become embittered and leave Jewish education. Committee meetings become monthly battlegrounds. *If we don't learn to work together we will not succeed individually.*

What I have learned in my experience is that most parents and educators want the same thing: continuity for their children and in the Jewish community today. This book is one attempt to bring the families and educators together. students. Affiliated families love Judaism as much as the educators who serve the tradition. Somehow we all lose sight of this commonality. More importantly, neither the school nor the family can achieve this goal alone – they must work in tandem. The first step in this process is for each to understand the other; the relationship should not be adversarial.

What is Continuity?

Years ago, when our town was embroiled in a religious issue that threatened to divide the community, the local Episcopal priest and I exchanged pulpits for a weekend. Our goal was to give each other's congregation an idea of how they were perceived by the outside world. On Friday night the priest almost caused a riot by criticizing us as a "one-issue" community.

"All you ever talk about is the Holocaust. Don't you realize that it happened fifty years ago? When will you get past it?"

With more than several survivors in the sanctuary, he could not understand what he had said to get everyone so angry. Yet, on some level his point must be considered. How do our children perceive their Jewish identity? When Emil Fackenheim exhorted the community to remain Jewish so as not to "Give Hitler a posthumous victory," we were living in the aftermath of the Holocaust. Today's students, two generations removed, need other reasons to be Jewish. They need to understand our history but they also need to derive joy from it. This brings us to the heart of the matter. "Why do parents want a Jewish education for their children?" My experience suggests three possible answers:

1. Tradition! A *Bar/Bat Mitzvah* is necessary in the Jewish community. As we became *B'nai Mitzvah,* so should our children.

2. Tradition! We want our children to know about the history of our people. We want them to know how we have suffered and appreciate how good we have it today

3. Meaning. We are affiliated because it means something to us. We want to be involved in the Jewish community and we want our children to share in the involvement. We want them to be comfortable in Jewish settings.

In the movie *Fiddler on the Roof,* when Tevye asks "Why do we wear a prayer shawl?" and answers "I don't know, but *it's a tradition,*" He advocates ignorance as a positive Jewish value, you do it because it is a tradition. Do we really want our children to have Tevye's "raging thirst" for knowledge? Tradition is not a reason to give our children a Jewish education. Wanting to teach our children because that is our tradition is not the way to go – it doesn't work.

A child learns to love and have compassion by being taught in a way that promotes love and compassion. While our children need to learn about our history – they must also learn to love the feel of a *Tallit* in prayer, to value the person in need as a full-fledged member of our community deserving our attention and support, to recognize that being Jewish means a lifelong relationship with *Tikun Olam* (fixing the world) and that every action no matter how seemingly insignificant is of great importance to us, to the world and to God.

> *The reason for Jewish law is to train us how to act in familiar situations so that when we find ourselves in uncharted territory, we have enough experience to know what is expected of us.*
> *(Yitzchak Arama, Commentary on Leviticus)*

Chapter 3: What Are Your Values? And Do You Share Them With Your Children?

Ask the average person which is more important to him, making money or being devoted to his family? Virtually everyone will answer "family" without hesitation. But, watch how the average person actually lives out his life. See where he really invests his time and energy. He will give away the fact that he does not really live by what he says he believes. (Harold Kushner)

Our tradition is practical. We are judged by our actions, not our intentions.[3] We all have impure thoughts but as long as we don't act upon our baser instincts, we have no need for guilt or atonement. As long as our actions are good so are we. However, this works both ways. While we are not held responsible for the sins we only *wish* to commit, we don't get credit for those things not begun. No matter how good the intention, if we don't actually take the time to be with our kids, we are not parenting.

I am reminded of the story of the little girl who asked her mother:
"Mommy, where do we go when we die?"
"Everyone goes to heaven."
"Daddy can't go, he won't leave the office."

Children model their parents. This means that as parents, we must take an active role in our children's education. We must also be the educators. For this we have to leave the office. We have to be clear as to our values.

The Giraffe Project[4] teaches that the fundamental questions in each child's education should be: Who are your heroes? If you asked

---

[3] Everyone over a certain age will remember Jimmy Carter's interview in Playboy magazine in which he admitted that he had "committed adultery in his heart" many times. The press went wild. How could a presidential candidate say this? What type of person could he be? Yet, the Jewish community, figuratively, scratched its head. What was the big deal? He only "thought" about it. He didn't "do" anything.

[4] To learn more about the Giraffe Project, check out the website: www.giraffe.org

your children to list five of their *heroes*, who would make that list? Would it be sports figures, rock stars or actors? Would it be the people who adorn the *Teen People* magazine or *Sports Illustrated*? For that matter, who are **your** heroes? If *their* list would not satisfy you, would **your** list satisfy you? And, would your children know who your heroes are? How?

People often confuse the word *hero* with the word *star*. The dictionary tells us that a hero is "a person admired for their achievements and accomplishments, a person who shows great courage." A star is a person who "is widely known and referred to often." A star is a person with unique talents, someone who can perform feats that very few can duplicate. They become celebrities because of this talent. But, they are **not** heroes.

As a pulpit rabbi I often find myself sitting with families who have lost a loved one. As I listen to their stories, sometimes there is laughter with the tears. Through these stories I can see the legacy of love and values that will survive the loss. But far too often my experience is different. Sometimes there are no stories and the values to be passed on are missing. I have stopped counting how many times an adult child has regretted their inability to have been able to talk to their parents, how many times the parent/child bond was only defined by watching football on Sunday afternoons or talking sports, buying clothing and dressing up. I have heard too many lives encapsulated as being "impeccably dressed" or "classy." In too many cases this is all the survivors are left with; the deceased has left behind no stories or memories. For what will they be remembered? What footprints have they left behind?

Home Work:

Activity: Have a family discussion: If you could invite any three people to dinner (past, present, future, fictional or real) who would they be? Why?

Community Voices
*The (Not So) Secret World Of Grandparents:
One Grand-Family's Tikun Olam Tale*
By: Sharon Halper[5]

Grandparents are champions, co-conspirators, mentors, genies, coaches, supporters and historians for their grandchildren. Ideally, a grandparent is someone who combines their life experience modified by their personal style in creating a multi generational relationship crowned with unconditional love. A grandparent's life experiences can hone their priorities, and the complexity of the striving of earlier years often gives way to contentment and perhaps even wisdom.

The essential question most often asked is, "What will my children and grandchildren *have* because of me?" But, perhaps it should become "Who will my children and grandchildren **be** because of me?" Perhaps the concern for acquisition and monetary inheritance should give way to a wish for transmission and an ethical legacy. This can be accomplished by opening the windows of the world to grandchildren; the world of what has been through family stories and traditions, the world we know through events and adventures, the world of what might be through the use of imagina-tion and the world that can be created together by joining who we are and who we wish to be.

What follows is this grandmother's story entitled "Praying in the Mattress Store."

I can still remember a basic lesson in moral education that took place at the kitchen table of my childhood ... *'There are children starving*

---

[5] Sharon Halper has spent nearly three decades in the field of Jewish Education, most recently serving as the Regional Educator for the New Jersey-West Hudson Valley Council of the Union for Reform Judaism and is the first Regional *Tikkun Olam* Fellow. She has served as a Congregational Director of Education, and Teacher and Director of the Melton Adult Mini-School in Rockland County, NY. She has authored several publications, among them *To Learn Is To Do* and *Holy Days Holy Ways*, both for the URJ Press. She served as Editor for the 'Torah in Action' component of the new URJ *Parasha* study guides, intended to encourage *B'nai Mitzvah* students to bring the *Mitzvot* of their Torah portions into their lives.

in Europe' ... a statement that encompassed both the actuality of my parents' experiences and my rejection of whatever was on the day's menu. Far from the reality of the circumstances, I suspect that I was left loaded both with guilt **and** the dreaded vegetable.

In an age of wide-screen wars, larger-than-life faces of starving children in Africa and magazine covers of waves of refugees fleeing every horror imaginable, many of us, the children who would have wished to send their serving of vegetables to Europe, look at their children's children and wonder how we make the reality of the world and their potential contributions authentic.

And so it was, when we had the opportunity to spend some time in rural, devastated Mississippi, bringing aid to the now nearly forgotten victims of Hurricane Katrina, there was no question that my husband David and I would bring our 11–year old grandson with us. Our hope was that for grandson Alex and his generation, their contribution to alleviating the suffering of the world would go beyond their particular portion of vegetables and a dose of guilt delivered with every seemingly under appreciated privilege.

There is no certainty that our venture will matter or that we will be able to see how it might have, but if I could wish for and communicate to our grandsons and their generation, *I would want them to know...*

... they each matter.
> In ways that we cannot begin to imagine, we can bring joy to others and meaning to our own lives.
>
> *May they seize opportunities to matter to someone.*

... our choices make our lives.
> The people in our group who schlepped cartons over the skids that served as pathways through the swampy relief distribution center might have spent the week behind their desks or basking on a beach. Instead they escaped the snow for the mud and gnats of Mississippi.
>
> *May our children and grandchildren make meaningful choices.*

... life is abundant with blessings.

As we stood with a woman who had spent two years in a FEMA trailer, adequate for a week's vacation but abysmal as a home, she proclaimed "Ain't nothin' the good Lord takes away from you that He don't give back." And when the group with which we traveled concluded a purchase of dozens of mattresses for people who had been sleeping on the floor for years, the salesman asked if we could pray. Far from our homes and traditions – and somewhat startled by the impromptu creation of this retail sanctuary - we stood as a lusty blessing was offered for our presence and for our welfare.

May our children – and theirs - always be able to recognize the blessings of life that are arrayed before them.

... you are what you do when you aren't doing what you have to do to pay the bills.

When we met them, the farmers from Illinois who were in Mississippi for periods ranging from two weeks to three months, were dry-walling the future home of a family of five that had been living in a FEMA trailer.

May we all learn to offer our admiration wisely.

... we need one another.

Separated by geography and culture, age, religion or race, we are united in our commonality. Then will our children and grandchildren come to be called *Rachamim B'nai Rachamim*, "compassionate children of compassionate ancestors."

SIMPLE IDEAS FOR HERE AND NOW

Grandparents can supply "food" for their grandchild's moral imagination – the part of them that envisions how they can make a difference – by modeling values-based celebrations:

1. Calculate the cost of a holiday dinner that you prepare and symbolically invite "guests" to your observance. Grandchildren can help with the math and with determining the

recipients of the donation to alleviate hunger.
2. Share birthdays or Chanukah by purchasing one of a grandchild's favorite items for donation to a child in a shelter. Your grandchild will never forget that somewhere someone is enjoying a pair of their favorite sneakers or reading their favorite book.
3. If you shop together, allocate a sum for a grandchild to spend for donations to a local food bank. Encourage comparison shopping and making wise decision-making. Remember also that those who are in need enjoy the same things that we all do! So if your grandchild has a passion for M&M's, it is likely that other kids, even those who rely on a food bank, would also enjoy M&M's.
4. Accompany gifts of money by a percentage for *Tzedakah* donation. Provide information about recipients of your personal *Tzedakah* as a way of expanding your grandchild's *Tzedakah*-giving horizons.
5. Teach your grandchild a skill and practice it together if proximity allows. Knit or crochet hats or scarves for children on Indian reservations or blankets for babies in family shelters. For young grandchildren, purchase fleece fabric and cut fringes on two sides. Children can knot the fringes as pairs or in a pattern of their creation, resulting in a scarf, shawl or blanket for donation to a local organization.

Chapter 4. The Vocabulary of the Jewish Community: What Does It Mean To Be A Covenant Community?

*The purpose of the laws of the Torah...is to bring mercy,
loving-kindness and peace upon the world.
(Maimonides, Mishnah Torah Shabbat 2:3)*

*(In this world we sometimes) forget our own goodness...It
is not our expertise or skill that will restore the world.
The future may depend less on our expertise than on our
faithfulness. (Rachel Naomi Remen)*

The word *Tzedakah* can be translated in different ways. Some translate it as "charity" others as "the right thing to do." I choose to translate it as "rightful giving." This captures both the obligatory nature and the object (people in need) of the action.

In the workshops about *Tzedakah* that I have led through the years, I almost always start out with the question, "Why do we do *Tzedakah*?" You would be surprised at the responses I get from this simple fundamental question. They include:

1. As Jews we are supposed to help those in need.
2. Helping others is the highest goal we can aspire to.
3. By helping others we help ourselves.
4. It makes me feel good.
5. It's a value we are taught to practice.

While all these answers are valid, they are not right. The correct answer is, "We do *Tzedakah* because it is a *Mitzvah*." It is ironic that most people do not connect the action of *Tzedakah* with the concept of *Mitzvah*. It is troubling that, once this answer is given, no one seems to know what to do with it.

Most people think a *Mitzvah* is a "good deed." While that may be the common understanding of the term it is not accurate. The word *Mitzvah* means "commandment." Of course, your understanding of the term "commandment" depends upon whether you are "traditional" or "liberal."[6]

Mitzvah is a concept directly linked to the term Covenant, which is our formalized relationship with God. Each movement within Judaism avers that we are a "Covenantal People." However, just as each movement understands our relationship with God differently, each views the "Covenant" differently. You cannot decipher the differences between traditional and liberal unless you learn the differences of this religious vocabulary.[7]

A Traditional View of Covenant:

A traditional Jew believes that God gave the *Torah* to the entire Jewish people at Mount Sinai. God gave both the "Written *Torah*," which consists of the Five Books of Moses and the "Oral *Torah*," which consists of the *Talmud*. Both the Written and Oral *Torah* are the foundations of Jewish belief and thought. They can be interpreted by the legitimate decision-makers of Jewish law (rabbis) within specific rules of interpretation set down in the tradition.

The *Torah* is the personification of the Covenant which is binding to all Jews. It may be broken but it can never be abrogated. It is the eternal gift given to us. The Covenant requires us to acknowledge and be loyal to God. We do this by performing the *Mitzvot*, which are mandatory. When a traditional Jew gives Tzedakah, s/he performs the *Mitzvah* because it is required.

The Covenant is reciprocal. In return, God promises to protect the Jewish people and give us a homeland.

---

[6] I use the terms "liberal" and "traditional" instead of naming movements because in today's Jewish community there is no homogeneous belief within any movement. Orthodoxy and much of Conservative Judaism would fall into the traditional category and Reform, Reconstructionist and part of Conservative Judaism would fall in the liberal camp. However, I have met Orthodox Jews whose theology is liberal and Reform Jews whose theology is traditional.

[7] I would add that this is one of the main reasons why traditional Jews have such a hard time understanding liberal Jews and vice versa. Liberal Jews view observance as "restrictive" while traditional Jews view it as "liberating." Each does not understand the other which leads to miscommunication and distrust between the movements.

> *If there were not a special relationship based upon the Covenant, the Jewish people would have been happy to accept Uganda as the homeland as it was offered to them by the British in the early 1900's.*
>
> *There is a story told of Chaim Weitzman, the first President of Israel:*
>
> *Asked by a member of a British commission why the Jews would not accept another country in lieu of Palestine as their homeland, he answered:*
>
> *"Sir, that is like my asking you why you traveled thirty miles to see your own mother last week. After all, there are many kind, elderly matrons living much closer to you. Why did you not visit one of them instead?"*
>
> *"But she is my mother!"*
>
> *"So is Israel to the Jews," answered Weitzman.*

A Liberal View of Covenant:

A liberal view of the Covenant assumes that the *Torah* is not of Divine origin. God was not revealed at Mount Sinai and did not give the Israelites the *Torah*. Jewish tradition is based upon people in each generation striving to understand their relationship with God. People wrote the *Torah*, which was created from legends, oral traditions and the aspirations of the authors.

God serves as a source of inspiration, an ideal towards which we strive. It is our attempt to define God that gives our lives meaning and purpose. By striving to understand God's will, performing *Mitzvot*, dedicating ourselves to our tradition and our experience as Jews, we learn about God and ourselves.

If the *Torah* is the product of the encounter between people and God, then our devotion to doing what we understand as God's will, and the way we express it, creates a "relationship" between us that results in the Covenant. We become part of this Covenant because we wish to do God's will, to be part of such a community, to be part of the history of a people who have chosen to do so. Ultimately, it is the individual's interpretation of this relationship which determines their place in the

Covenant.

A Traditional Look at the Concept of *Mitzvah*:

Mitzvot are given for a reason. While we may not always understand the rationale for all the *Mitzvot*, we believe that they are vital to our mission as Jews.

> *For what does it matter to the Holy One, Blessed be He whether or not the Jews carry out the laws of Kashrut? It is clear then that the commandments were given solely for the purpose of training the people.*
> (Midrash Tanchumah, Shmini 7)

Just as athletes must train to excel in sports, we must perform *Mitzvot* to train us to do God's work. Doing *Mitzvot* helps us to become better Jews.

A Liberal View of the Concept of *Mitzvah*:

A *Mitzvah* is our attempt to become closer to God. Some *Mitzvot* are done with a group and others are done alone, all have the potential to bring us closer to God.

As Jews we are free to make choices and decide which *Mitzvot* add meaning to our lives and which do not. We are given the authority over our personal actions and beliefs. But authority carries with it responsibility. We have the responsibility to make educated choices about our performance of *Mitzvot*. That means not only learning and trying, but also adapting or adopting certain actions that are meaningful in our search for an understanding of God.

We may spend our entire lives in search of our Jewish identity. The meaning is in the journey, not necessarily the journey's end.

Covenant + Commandment = Community

Our community is created by the combined elements of Covenant and Commandment. To put it another way, our relationship with God determines how we relate to one another. The *Torah* is our guide; we learn about Covenant, Commandment and Community from studying the narratives and laws of the *Torah*. Two examples from the book of Genesis illustrate this:

> *Cain spoke to his brother Abel. When they were in the field, Cain rose over his brother Abel and killed him. God said to Cain, "Where is your brother Abel?"*
> *(Genesis 4:8-9)*

There are few more memorable verses in the *Torah*. Cain condemns himself with the admission that he really doesn't care about his brother. He becomes the eternal wanderer because he doesn't understand the interconnectedness of community.

Contrast this with the ending of the Joseph story:

> *Joseph could no longer control himself in front of those who stood with him. He called, "Let all before me leave."*
> *No one stood with him when he identified himself to his brothers. He raised his voice in tears. Egypt heard. The house of Pharaoh heard. Joseph said to his brothers,*
> *"I am Joseph, is my father yet alive?" His brothers could not answer him because they were afraid of him. Joseph said to his brothers, "Come close to me." They did. He said, "I am Joseph your brother whom you sold down to Egypt. Do not be worried or angry that you sold me here, for God sent me here to keep me alive..."* *(Genesis 45:1-4)*

Joseph rises to the second most powerful position in Egypt years after his brothers have sold him to slavery. Somehow, he has been able to forgive them and recognize that his position should be used to save his family/community – and that he is the only one who can. We have seen similar dynamics with the rescue and acceptance of various Jewish populations from around the world to Israel. It may have taken the Jewish community years to form a united plan of action, but once committed thousands of Jews from Ethiopia, the Former Soviet Union, Yemen, Syria, Iraq and other countries have found a home.

The process has not been easy: economics, identity, assimilation are all issues of great import, yet we always recognized a responsibility towards them. They are part of our community, our Covenant community.

> *Some people were sitting in a ship when one of them took a drill and began to bore a hole under his seat. The other passengers protested to him, "What are you doing?" He said to them, "What has this to do with you? Am I not boring a hole under my own seat?" They retorted, "But the water will come in and drown us all." Vayikra Rabbah 4:6)*

Remember, the wicked son of the *Haggadah* asks, "What are these observances to you?" He says, "you" not "we." Thus he excluded himself from the community. Had he been in Egypt, he would not have been redeemed.

Why Do We Need This Vocabulary?

Without the foundational belief that *Tzedakah* is a Covenantal *Mitzvah* it remains just something to do that will "make you feel good," nothing more than a voluntary act.

How do you impress upon your children the need to help others when it is only voluntary?

> *Whoever can stop the people of their city from sinning but does not...is held responsible for the sins of the people of their city. If he can stop the whole world from sinning and does not, they are held responsible for the sins of the whole world.* (Shabbat 54b)

Home Work:

1. To better understand the concept of Covenant, discuss all the relationships we have in our lives. Think about a very important relationship in your life in that you and another person share a covenant, even if you've never talked about it. Talk about the obligations of a parent/child, child/parent, husband/wife, and student/teacher.
2. To better understand the concept of *Mitzvah*, discuss what you "hear" when you study the following text:

Text	What Do I hear?	What Must I Do?
Each of you will revere his mother and father and keep my Sabbaths. I the Lord am your God. *(Leviticus 19:3)*		
You shall not pick your vineyard bare, or gather the fallen fruit of your vineyard. You shall leaven them for the poor and stranger. I the Lord am your God. *(Leviticus 19:10)*		
You shall not insult the deaf, or place a stumbling block before the blind. You shall fear your God. I am the Lord. *(Leviticus 19:14)*		
There shall be no needy among you – since the Lord your God will bless you in the land which the Lord your God is giving you as a hereditary portion. *(Leviticus 15:4)*		

3. Read Chapter Two, entitled, "Always Tag All Four Bases" of Joel Grishaver's book, *40 Things You Can Do To Save the Jewish People*.

Story:

"I will tell you a parable," said Rabbi Akiva. Once while walking beside a river, a fox saw some fish jumping up and down in the water, in evident panic.

The fox asked, "Why are you in a panic? Who are you running from?"

They said, "There are fisherman in the lake. They are throwing nets to catch us. We are running away from them."

The fox said, "Come up on the dry land. There are no nets at all here, and I promise that I will protect you."

The fish said, "Foolish fox. We are afraid of the fisherman, who is a danger to us in our home. How much more would we have to fear from you on the land, where we are not at home and cannot survive?"

Rabbi Akiva continued. "So it is with the Jews. While we may suffer because of our love for the Torah, we cannot survive unless we keep the Torah near us and don't forsake it."

(Berakhot 61b)

Section Two: Mitzvot

The last section ended with the statement that, "Without the foundational belief that *Tzedakah* is a Covenantal *Mitzvah* it remains just something to do that will make you feel good, nothing more than a voluntary act." *Mitzvot* are the actions that reflect our communal values.

This section discusses a selection of *Mitzvot* that exemplify our communal values towards those in need. They represent our community at its best.

There is an apocryphal story about a car stopped on a freeway, its owner, wearing a *Kippah* (skullcap) is standing alone next to the flat tire. A car stops and another man wearing a *Kippah* gets out and helps him fix the flat. As they part, the Good Samaritan[8] asks "Which synagogue do you belong to?" The answer is, "Oh, I'm not Jewish. I keep the *Kippah* in my glove compartment in case of an emergency. I know that if I put it on, someone will stop to help me."

Jewish humor always has a bit of truth to it. We do tend to look after our own. You will see, though, that some of the Good People outlined in these chapters are not Jewish and nearly all of the Good People have worked with non Jews. It is our challenge to help the world see that a person in need has no nationality. Everyone is our kin. In this way, and in this way only, can we be sure of completing the task of *Tikun Olam*.

---

[8] The use of the phrase "Good Samaritan" is pure irony. The story of the Good Samaritan is from the Christian Bible, used to describe a situation where a shunned person turns out to be the most ethical. Currently this phrase is used to denote a stranger who stops to help in what we would call a random act of kindness.

Chapter 5: Feeding the Hungry - *Lechem LeR'evim*. How the Supermarket Aisles Can Teach Kids About Hunger

One who feeds the hungry feeds God also.
(Agadat Shir Hashirim)

A woman once told me that she despaired of the selfishness of her children. She could not understand how they turned out this way...we don't help people become generous by giving to them but by involving them as we give to others.
(Rachel Naomi Remen)

A Good Person: Clara Hammer

Clara is a New York City woman who emigrated to Jerusalem after retirement. One Friday morning she was waiting in line at her local butcher shop to buy some chickens for her *Shabbat* meal. *Shabbat*, tradition tells us, is a time when we set our best table – the best dishes and silver, a crisp clean tablecloth, perhaps even fresh flowers and candles – all to welcome the Sabbath Queen.

Clara noticed her butcher handing a young girl a large plastic bag filled with chicken skin and bones; parts of the chicken always discarded or fed to animals. When it was finally Clara's turn to get her order, she asked the butcher, "How many cats and dogs does that young girl have?"

The butcher, responded that what was in the bag was not for the youngster's pets, but, rather, for her family. The girl's father was very ill, her mother did not work, and they didn't have enough money to buy food for *Shabbat*. The butcher had been giving them food for a long time without asking for payment, but he could not continue doing that. So, every Friday morning the daughter came to the butcher shop to collect the skin and bones so that the family could at least make a soup for *Shabbat*

Horrified that anyone would be reduced to such circumstances, Clara instructed the butcher to give the girl's family two chickens and a pound of ground meat every *Shabbat*. She would pay the bill herself, anonymously.

Clara heard about more families in similar circumstances and she decided to help them, as well. That is how Clara Hammer became known as "The Chicken Lady of Jerusalem" and that is how her charity fund began. She is known worldwide for her passion to make sure that poor people can afford to celebrate *Shabbat*.

She receives money from *Bar* or *Bat Mitzvahs*, brides and grooms and others who want to share their *simcha* (happy occasions) with others who are less fortunate.[9] Today, even as Clara approaches her centennial birthday,* she provides over 100 families with food for their *Shabbat* table. Her yearly butcher bill is over $50,000.

*   *   *

Perhaps the greatest challenge to parents in teaching values to their children is how to have the greatest affect with the least effort. Parenting can be all consuming and the logistics of life can get in the way of teaching. It's also important to find a natural environment for teaching values. Lecturing does not work. For these reasons we start with the *Mitzvah* of "Feeding the Hungry." What could be more "natural" than asking your six year old to go shopping (especially if they can pick out the ice cream), and while there – help those in need as well.

Yom Kippur is the holiest day of the year. Its dominant theme is atonement. Through atonement we achieve forgiveness for our sins and are given an opportunity to "clean the slate" of our transgressions. The *Torah* orders us to "afflict our souls" on *Yom Kippur*, perhaps so that we can better understand the suffering we have caused others. The *Torah* only commands the affliction of soul; it does not specify how to do so. The Rabbis define the affliction as fasting; the first among all other restrictions for that day. If the definition of suffering in our tradition is fasting, then anyone who does not have enough to eat is suffering – and we are required to feed them. Perhaps if we can feel the hunger we can empathize with those to whom every day seems like a *Yom Kippur*.

---

[9] Believe it or not, everyone who sends her money gets a personal thank you note written by Clara herself.

* As this book went to press, we were sorry to learn of Clara's death.

There is a story told by *Nachum, Ish Gamzu*,[10] one of the teachers of Rabbi *Akiva*:

I was once traveling to the house of my father-in-law, taking with me three donkeys – loads of food and drink. A starving man asked me for food. I answered that I would give him some when I unloaded, but before I could do so, he fell dead.

I greatly grieved over his death, and prayed that the Lord send sufferings upon me in expiation for my sin. I should not have delayed my help, but should have cut through the load and given him food at once.
(Ta'anit, 21)

According to the *Shulchan Arukh*,[11] the code of Jewish law, if a person comes and asks you for money you are not required to give it to him. There is an understanding that the money might or might not be used in an appropriate way (will the person buy alcohol or drugs with it? You don't know). However, if they ask you for food, no matter if they are dressed in a Brooks Brothers suit or Manolo Blahnick shoes, you must feed them. Of all the commandments we are given, feeding the hungry takes priority over them all.

And we all know someone who is hungry. Anyone who tells you that they don't know a person who is hungry is simply not aware. Just because someone lives in an upper middle class suburban setting and owns their own home does not indicate the life they lead inside. I know people in large homes who don't have enough money to eat properly. And, even if you don't like their priorities; putting appearances ahead of food, Jewish law comes to remind us that it is not for us to judge them – only to feed them.

---

[10] The phrase, "*Ish Gamzu*" can mean "a man from *Gamzu*," or "the man who says '*gamzu*.'" The word "*gamzu*" literally means "this too." *Nahum* is reputed to have been called "a man who says '*gamzu*,'" because no matter what happened he always responded, "*gam zu litovah*," meaning "this is also for the good." Perhaps his name suggests how he resolved the story above.

[11] *Yoreh Deah* 251:10ff and discussion in the commentaries.

Home Work:

1. Start a canned food collection drive at home. Place a food basket in or around the kitchen and have each member take turns placing one item of food in it before each meal. When it is full take it to a food pantry.
2. Each time you go shopping, especially with your children, allow them to pick out one item of food to buy for the hungry. And remember it is o.k., from time to time, to select a bag of candy or chips.
3. Make a family habit of cutting coupons from the Sunday paper and bring them when you shop. Bring the coupons to a local food bank or send them to an appropriate shelter.

<u>Story</u>

The leaders of the Jewish community met to decide what to do about the large number of poor strangers who came into the city begging for funds. At the mass meeting, the leaders concluded that only closing the city to poor strangers would prevent their placing an economic burden on the city.

The Vilna Gaon had been invited to the meeting without knowing its purpose. The great scholar had interrupted his studies for what he had been told was an important matter. When he heard the suggestion to close the city to the poor wandering Jews, the Gaon sought out the head of the community.

"I'm sorry that I left the study of Torah for this meeting," said he.

"I told you that I did not wish to discuss community affairs except when a new custom is to be adopted for which there may not be a precedent."

"But that is exactly the case," said the president. "We are adopting a new custom; no community prohibits strangers from entering its gate."

"That is not new," the Gaon said, "Indeed it is one of the oldest customs in history. Do you not remember that it was the custom of Sodom and Gomorrah not to let strangers enter?"

The poor continued to be allowed to enter the city.

Chapter 6: Respect For Elders - *L'hader Pnai Zaken*
Caring For Elders Is Not a Visit With Grandma

The Kotsker Rebbe gathered his disciples and asked, "Where is God?" "His glory fills the universe," was their astonished exclamation. "No, my sons, that is the answer for the angels. For us, the answer is, the Presence of God is where He is permitted to enter."

It can be said of young children as it has been said of the elderly, that they need so little from us but they need that little so much. (Rachel Naomi Remen)

A Good Person: Dr. William Thomas

Dr. William Thomas has come up with something that reduces his patients' rate of infection by 50%, need for medications by 50% and their death rate by 25%. You could say he planted a Garden of Eden.

When Thomas got his Harvard medical degree, he wasn't planning on a specialty in geriatrics, but he found himself medical director of a large nursing home in upstate New York. It was so close to his home, he could bicycle to work and make a good living.

But Thomas soon saw that he wasn't helping. He learned why the studies showed that people would rather die than go to a nursing home. Nursing homes, including the one he ran, were sterile, barren places that cut elders off from all signs of life. He saw why an alarming number of nursing home residents die for the wrong reasons – they succumb not to diseases but to loneliness and despair.

Thomas made changes to improve their lives, but these changes created conflict with established procedure and State law.

He risked being fined and possible expulsion from the practice of medicine, for "professional misconduct." He ignored certain accepted procedures for treating the elderly. For example, where State law allowed for only one animal in the entire home he brought in parakeets, dogs and cats; 137 animals in total. He filled elders' rooms with growing plants that they cared for along with their pets. He turned the lawns into tilled patches where residents could grow their favorite vegetables. He also added a chicken coop and a rabbit hutch. As the residents began to exert greater control on aspects of their lives, their lives began to improve.

Children were added. An on-site daycare center was built and kids spilled into the elders' rooms for visits. Older children arrived after school to spend their afternoons at the home instead of going home to empty homes. "The Eden Alternative" was taking shape.

Today hundreds of nursing homes have "Edenized," changing from "dead zones" into lively, nurturing, happier places where elders are thriving. "Most nursing homes would make a desert look great," says Thomas. "What they offer people is loneliness, helplessness and boredom…It's all happening because of the new environment nursing homes are creating."

*   *   *

In the first quote of this chapter I noted that the Kotsker Rebbe taught that God exists where we allow God to enter. I wonder if the Kotsker Rebbe would say that God is present in nursing homes?

One of the most valuable lessons a child can learn is that every action, no matter how seemingly mundane carries with it a spark of holiness. Each interaction is imbued with the possibility of *Mitzvah*. This is never more evident than our interaction with elderly people. First though, we have to sensitize our children (and perhaps ourselves) to what it really means to be old in our society.

Try an experiment. If your children are *Bar/Bat Mitzvah* age or under, ask them the following questions:
1. What makes your grandparents happy?
2. What makes your grandparents sad?
3. What makes your grandparents afraid?

Every time I have asked these questions of children, without exception most answer:
1. My grandparents are happy when they visit us.
2. They are sad when we are not with them.
3. They are not afraid.

Children are by nature self-centered and are not to be blamed if these are their answers, especially because grandparents tend to dote on grandchildren and help sustain this self-centeredness. We live in a society in which family members often live at great distances from each other. It is not unusual for grandparents to live far from their grandchildren and so a result is visits are infrequent. Phone contact and internet is a primary source of communication. But, you cannot give virtual hugs.

Grandparents do not really want to "live" in front of their grandchildren. What profit is there in telling them about their doctor's visits, their driving experiences, or their aches and pains?

It is likely that the only meaningful contact our children may have had with the elderly in our community comes from their grandparents. Our children don't know what elderly people are like. By giving our children a limited and largely unrealistic picture of old age, how can we expect them to reconcile the elderly that they do see? What message are we giving them when we take them to nursing homes for *Mitzvah* projects?

We do our children a disservice by not trusting them with life experiences. When did they become unable to handle mature issues of life? When did we decide they were too delicate to know about the aging process?

> *It is natural for old people to be despised by the general population when they can no longer function as they once did, but sit idle, and have no purpose. The commandment, "Honor your father and your mother" was given specifically for this situation.*
> *(Gur Aryeh Halevi)*

My father's grandmother (my great-grandmother) was the perfect model of the Wicked Witch of the West. She wore black; black stockings, black dress, black shoes. She wore her silver hair in a bun. She had a humungous wart on her chin with two black hairs growing out of it. She mumbled all the time. I was petrified of her. She couldn't have been more than sixty. My parents would go visit her, but they wouldn't tell me where we were going until they parked the car at her apartment.

What astonished me was that my father loved her. He loved being with her. Even as a child of four or five, even though I was scared to death that she would look at me, I knew that he adored her – and she him. As a child of six or seven, I was even more astonished that my mother loved her. Only years later did I learn that while my father's mother (his father had died years before) and family were against my parent's marriage, only his grandmother (my great-grandmother) stood by them during those hard times (and they were hard times). She was a woman of quality – and I eventually saw her as such but only long after she herself had died.

I learned a lot through that interaction. Perhaps it was a lesson I didn't realize I had learned until I was an adult, but it was an important lesson nonetheless. I look back now and realize how much I would have missed; learning about my parents and life, if I didn't have these memories.

> *Honor and respect the aged and saintly scholar whose physical powers are broken, equally with the young and vigorous one; for the broken tablets of stone no less than the whole ones had a place in the Ark of the Covenant.*
> *(Berakhot 8b)*

Respecting the aged of any community is a very important *Mitzvah*. In some ways the community is judged by how it treats those whose bodies have betrayed them. But, what does it mean to respect? How does one "respect" an "elder?"

First and foremost you recognize their humanity. They are not *objects* to be manipulated. They are not *obstacles* to be dealt with. They are *human beings,* each with a unique past and present. They are individuals who may no longer be functional or useful as we define those terms – but they are not baggage to be moved at our convenience.

Second; be patient and compassionate. It's true that when confronted with a person who must wear a diaper, is incapable of independent motion, garbles their speech and needs to be fed that we become frustrated. Somehow, though, we have the ability to overcome this when it comes to babies. And, we love babies.

So why not the elderly?

Home Work:

1. Have your children call their grandparents and interview them about their lives. Help them formulate the questions to ask. Remember to prep your parents before the call!
2. Take a child to a nursing home and both of you read different parts of the newspaper to someone who is visually impaired. Make sure the material is interesting.
3. Locate a local nursing home and ask the activities director to give you a list of "wishes" from some of the residents (particularly those who may not have visitors very often). Have your children discuss ways to make some of the "wishes" come true.

<u>Story:</u>

The little girl saw her mother angrily give her grandmother a wooden spoon and bowl at the dinner table.

"Why does grandma get a wooden bowl and spoon?"

"Because she breaks things. She can't hold on. I want to give her something that she will not destroy," came the exasperated reply.

The child said, "Mommy, you have to keep that bowl and spoon safe."

"Why?"

"Well, when grandma dies, I will need them for you someday."

Chapter 7: Refraining From Evil Language –*Lashon Harah*
Sticks & Stones: Names Hurt More

*Judge a person not according to the words of his mother,
but according to the comments of his neighbors.
(Midrash Tehillim 48:2)*

*Sticks and stones may break our bones, but words
will break our hearts. (Robert Fulghum)*

A Good Person: Neto Villareal

In Marsing, Idaho, high school football is everything. On Friday nights, hundreds of people from the town and the nearby farms come to watch the Marsing Huskies play. They cheer when things go good and jeer when things are not. If you were a Latino, the jeers were "Stupid Mexican!" and other unmentionable statements. The hecklers were not students or even the opposing team's supporters, they were from the Marsing parents and adults who came to watch the games.

Neto Villareal was a star Husky who had a future in college football. However he considered aborting his high school career because the insults were hurtful and wrong. It was wrong that these "fans" were hurling insults and using language that was meant to injure. He organized the other Hispanic players and they decided that until the insults stopped they would not play.

His coach and the principal were not supportive. They warned him that their actions would make things worse and anger more people. At this point most of the Hispanic players gave up and agreed to play. Neto alone approached the school board aware that one of them was guilty of using the foul language Neto was fighting against. He told them that he would refuse to play if the insults did not stop. "Now," he explained, "They can't say nobody told them."

The student body president was inspired by Neto's courage and persistence. He wrote a letter on behalf of all the students, asking adults to stop the insults or be ejected from the stadium.

The next football game was homecoming, the most important game of the season complete with a parade, music and floats. The students wanted the principal to read their letter before the game on behalf of all the students. The principal refused. Neto and his allies went to the school superintendent, who gave permission for a student to read the letter.

When the stadium was full and the game was about to begin, a student called for everyone's attention and read the letter over the loudspeaker. When she finished there was silence. Then the people stood up and cheered. Hearing the crowd's roaring agreement to end the insults, Neto Villareal came back on the field to play, though in ways that really count, he had already won.

*   *   *

If there was ever a *Mitzvah* that parents could model for children, it is this one. Hurtful language comes in many forms. When first married, both my wife and I had a tendency to use colorful inappropriate language upon occasion. We knew we had to stop when our first child was born because kids absorb everything – and we didn't want our three year old to become a parrot repeating our family conversations.

We thought ourselves very smart when we substituted euphemisms for the curses. Everything was fine until the Nursery School director called me one day to ask me why my daughter was calling her teacher a "diphthong," "and oh, by the way, what is a "diphthong?"

That day we learned that *Lashon Harah* has many permutations. Words used harmlessly in one context can be mimicked into hurtful barbs by another.

This *Mitzvah* is a fundamental building block of any community or family. Words are our primary form of commun- ication; they can build or destroy relationships. Most people think of *Lashon Harah* as being "evil gossip." Technically, according to Jewish law, *Lashon Harah* is when you tell the truth about someone in a disparaging way.

> *Everyone knows why a bride enters the bridal chamber. But if someone makes obscene comments about it, even if that person was destined for seventy years of happiness, the decree is changed to one of unhappiness.*
> (Shabbat 33a)

In my life as a rabbi, I have served in three congregations. Each pulpit was different; in *their needs* and *their expectations* of me as the rabbi. Each had a different dynamic that created unique challenges for me. In my second congregation I followed a rabbi who had been "retired to emeritus status." In effect, he was being paid to leave the congregation alone. I was brought in as his replacement to help heal the congregation and rebuild its programs. It was there that I learned the true meaning of *Lashon Harah*. I learned a basic truth in my three years there – every action can be viewed positively or negatively depending on the agenda of the observer.

For example, kindness to one person was interpreted as favoritism. Encouraging a young mother to enter the sanctuary to say *Kaddish* (the mourner's prayer) for her recently deceased father led to an accusation that I favored the younger group of congregants because I allowed her infant daughter to cry uninterrupted during the prayer. I stopped walking through the congregation during services when I was accused of ignoring a person I did not see and therefore did not greet. Each mistake was magnified. I also learned that some people are in so much pain they feel required to spread it around.

But the reverse is also true. Words can heal and bring a sense of common purpose and community.

> *It is said that Tolstoy, born to a wealthy aristocratic family, was always a friend to the poor. One day, approached by a beggar who asked for a kopeck, Tolstoy reached into his pocket – and could not even find even the smallest copper. He turned to the man and said:*
> *"Brother, I am sorry; I have nothing to give you."*
> *The man, tears in his eyes, replied, "But you have given me something. You called me brother."*

Tolstoy had nothing to share except kind words – yet they helped the person in need. Words are gifts that we give to others. In the right circumstance they are as important as money to a hungry person. *Lashon Harah* is the opposite of everything *Tzedakah* stands for. It robs a person of their dignity, which only adds to their hunger and need.

There are those who believe that the best way to combat *Lashon Harah* is to "rise above it" and ignore it. I have tried it – it doesn't work.

Maimonides views *Lashon Harah* as a sin that contributes to ruining the world (the exact opposite of *Tikun Olam*) because communication is what holds a community together. If members of a community cannot trust each other, the community does not exist.

Those who think *Lashon Harah* is harmless need look no further than the assassination of *Yitzchak Rabin*. Would he have been a target if his detractors had not plastered posters of him in a Nazi uniform because they disagreed with his peace initiatives? If the climate had not been so poisoned with words, would he have had to die?

How many of us living comfortable suburban lives still see evidence that others believe and circulate literature that decries the belief that Jews are evil?

Home Work:

1. Read and discuss the story "The Gossip" in the book *Who Knows Ten*.
2. Make a social contract at home that everyone will treat each other with respect.
3. Read the story of "The Great Debate" on page 315 of *Jewish*

Stories One Generation Tells Another by Peninnah Schram and discuss how it applies to this *Mitzvah*.
4. Play the game "telephone." Start the chain and watch how the phrase becomes fractured the longer it travels. Can you relate this activity to the *Mitzvah* of this lesson?
5. Read the fable entitled, "The Very Proper Gander" in James Thurber's *The Thurber Carnival* and discuss its relation to this *Mitzvah*.
6. Have your children share some examples of *Lashon Harah* from their own interactions with friends. Discuss how they might have responded differently.

Story:

The Nobel Prize is named after Alfred Nobel, the Swedish chemist who invented dynamite and made his fortune by licensing other governments to use this explosive for weapons. When Alfred Nobel's brother died, one newspaper accidentally printed an obituary for Alfred. It identified him as the inventor of dynamite, and the man who made it possible for armies to achieve new levels of mass destruction. Alfred Nobel was stunned to realize that his name would be forever associated with death and destruction.

Was this *Lashon Harah*? Why or why not.

Chapter 8: Visiting People Who Are Ill - *Bikur Cholim*
A Lesson in Humility

He who does not perform deeds of loving kindness is as one who has no God. (Avodah Zarah 17b)

Through illness people may come to know themselves for the first time and recognize not only who they genuinely are but also what really matters to them. (Rachel Naomi Remen)

Good People: Mike & Sue Turk

Mike and Sue Turk are a wonderful retired couple who have dual personalities. Most of the time they are loving parents and grandparents; they spend much of their time volunteering. But at certain times they change; their noses change color as do their faces, they put on mismatched clothing and make funny noises.

Sometimes, Mike and Sue become Buttercup and Sweetpea, *Mitzvah* clowns. Sue/Sweetpea might have blue hair, a large red nose, floppy ears and a very sad face. Mike/Buttercup sports a water-squirting flower in his lapel and tells very bad jokes. Because Sweetpea and Buttercup are *Mitzvah* clowns their job is to bring laughter and cheer to anyone who might be sick, or lonely or sad.

They visit children who are gravely ill. They bring toys to kids attached to tubes and machines. Some of these children lose their hair to chemotherapy. Each visit delivers balloon animals, stickers and buttons to bring smiles to small faces.

They target nursing homes where elderly residents laugh at their antics and jokes. Their most important work occurs when they lead workshops to teach adults and teens to become *Mitzvah* clowns.

*   *   *

You can be sure that *Bikur Cholim* is one *Mitzvah* that you will perform many times in your life. As we age and our friends and family get older, we will be called to visit hospitals with greater frequency. I still remember my first real visit to a hospital. I was twenty one years old when my father had open heart surgery. I went to see him in the recovery room – and he had the hiccups. He was stitched up and foggy; it was the first time I had ever seen my father in that condition, not really knowing where he was. He never remembered the visit, which was probably a good thing because I fainted and the nurses had to carry me out. The combination of seeing sutures down my father's chest and watching him, a World War II veteran of numerous combat missions over the South Pacific, completely helpless, was too much for me – even though I was an adult. Think of what happens in a hospital:

1. You usually only go there when you are sick.
2. Many people are in pain.
3. The patients wear funny and embarrassing outfits that sometimes don't cover their bodies.
4. You see the ones you love the most when they have the least control of their surroundings.
5. Sometimes you can't even use a bathroom.
6. People die there.
7. The food is not haute cuisine.
8. Little children are not allowed to visit.
9. People talk in hushed tones.
10. You have to be cheerful when you are scared.
11. It is a place filled with fear.
12. No one looks happy.

If you have never been a patient in a hospital, visiting the sick is one of the hardest tests of our values. No matter how much the staff try to make it a cheerful place, no matter how colorful the lobby, how up-to-date the restaurant, walking into a ward with room after room of sick people is stressful. It's a place that forces us to come face to face with our own frailty and reminds us that being in the hospital is a common fate that likely awaits us all.

If you have been a patient then you most likely realize how important visitors are. Hospital patients are truly "poor people."

> *Blessed is he who considers the poor (Psalms 41:1)*
> *Rav Huna said, "That is he who visits the sick."*
> *(Vayikra Rabbah 34:1)*

Rav Huna comes to teach us that there are different types of poverty. A person without money can be poor. Another can be poor without friends. And yet another can be poor without health. Lying in a hospital bed where your universe consists of walking circuits around a hallway, where your only view is other sick people is a form of poverty.

You have to be very careful how you act and appear in hospitals. For instance, you should not wear perfume or shaving cologne when visiting someone who is ill. Illness often heightens a person's sense of smell. Perfume can actually heighten their discomfort. You should not feel it necessary to talk with a patient all the time. You should not come near the patient, or sit on the bed, without asking permission. You have to be sure that you have positioned yourself so that the patient can see you and hear you without straining.

Despite all of this, we have to go to hospitals to visit. If we, as the visitors feel this way, how must the patients feel? We need to go because we are an intrinsic part of the healing process. It has been proven that people with strong ties to the "outside" world, people who are visited and cared for when they are in hospitals recover faster. People who are given the message "we miss you, we love you, come home soon" will do so. People who are optimistic and have a good support system live longer. If you care about someone and want them to get better, you must participate in their therapy.

Ironically, we usually associate the *Mitzvah* of *Bikkur Cholim* with hospitals and when a person leaves the hospital it is assumed that they have recovered. *Bikur Cholim* is not limited to visits to a hospital. People are also sick at home. The most important time to visit someone who is sick may be when they have returned home and their well-being is no longer on everyone's mind. In our society we respect a person's home as very private property, and we don't visit. Think though, of all the things you can do at a person's home (within reason) that you can't do at the hospital. You can bring a home cooked meal (check the dietary restrictions of course) or your dog (check allergies). To be sure, you don't want to overstay your welcome – but bringing that special personal touch can do wonders for a person's morale and recuperation.

When they are home, be sure to call first to arrange a visit, but call!

> *There is no limit as regards the visitation of the sick. What does this mean? Rav Yosef argued that it meant that there is "no limit" to its reward. Abaye said to him,*
> *"Is there a limit to the reward of any of the Mitzvot?"*
> *"The words 'no limit'," said Abaye "mean that (even) the great (people) must visit the small (insignificant) people."*
> *It once happened that one of Rabbi Akiva's disciples became ill, and none of the sages visited him. Then Rabbi Akiva himself went to the disciple's house, and because he saw to it that the floor was swept and sprinkled with water, the man recovered.*
> *"My master, you have restored me to life," the disciple said.*
> *Akiva went out and taught, "He who does not visit the sick is like someone who sheds blood." (Nedarim 39b – 40a)*

Reading between the lines we see that the *Talmud* records how uncomfortable even the sages were in visiting the sick. Discomfort is normal. That is why community models have to "lead" the way. Rabbi Akiva was the greatest scholar of his gener-ation. When he visited the sick, others were forced to as well.

Note that there is no status involved with this *Mitzvah*. We are divided up into two categories; those who are sick and those who must visit them. This is a unique *Mitzvah* because it is one which requires you to go somewhere, perhaps far away. Most other *Mitzvot* are performed at home, in congregations or school. *Bikur Cholim* requires a conscious move towards someone else.

It is also a *Mitzvah* that can be performed improperly.

> *A visitor came to see a sick man and asked him what ailed him. After the sick man told him, the visitor said: "Oh, my father died of the same disease." The sick man became extremely distressed, but the visitor continued, "Don't worry; I'll pray to God to heal you."*
>
> *To which the sick man answered: "And when you pray, add that I may be spared visits from any more stupid people."*
>
> (Voices of Wisdom p. 222)

Home Work:

1. Make up *Bikur Cholim* packages for Jews in local hospitals (for holidays or daily use). You can get ideas from the chaplain's office at the hospital or from those who have been patients. Use your imagination. Be creative.
2. Would you like to be a *Mitzvah* Clown? Contact Naomi Eisenberger at Naomi@goodpeoplefund.org for information on the nearest training site.
3. If you know someone who is ill, send a card or make a call to see how they are doing.
4. Find out what happens to leftover flowers from Shabbat services. Ask if you can rearrange them into small bouquets and deliver them to someone who may be ill at home or in the hospital.

Story:

Rabbi Beroka of Kuzistan often visited the market at Be Lapat. There he would meet Elijah the prophet.

"Does anybody in this market have a share in the world to come?" Rabbi Beroka asked one day...While they were talking, two men came by.

Elijah said, "Those two have a share in the world to come."

Rabbi Beroka went to them and said, "What do you do?"

They said, "We are jesters. When we see a person depressed or sick, we try to cheer him up. And when we see two people quarreling, we work hard to try to make peace between them." (Ta'anit 22a)

Community Voices
Bikur Cholim, Mitzvah Clowning, and Your Child's Self Esteem
By: Andrea Hirschfeld[12]

Clowning – a simple performance art. It is funny how it all started; you know, one thing often leads to the next. I was in our Rabbi's office when I happened to overhear him talking with friends of mine about needing someone to act as the administrator of a small grant they received to promote '*Mitzvah* Clowning' in New Jersey. I thought to myself, "Wait, I can do that for them. Sounds like fun." I knew the work they did as visiting pastoral clowns, and they were my friends, so how bad could it be?

To make a long story short, we involved others in my family to make a website, create promotional materials, and to help teach training seminars. In the end, I became a clown myself, *All Ears*, and my two daughters did as well, *Venus* and *Gingerbread*. But what really shocked me was my own reaction as I watched a group of sixth graders become completely transformed as they worked on assuming their own new clown identities and then take their acts on the road visiting the elderly at an assisted living residence. *I* had joined the *Mitzva*h Clowns because *I* loved my friends and wanted to spend time with them. After seeing what happened to the *children* who performed the *Mitzvah* of *Bikur Cholim* (visiting the sick), I couldn't deny the magic of *Mitzvot*. These kids had come straight from a long morning of Hebrew school. They brought in their little bag lunches and were noticeably bored through the first part of our class in which we taught the basis for *Mitzvah* clown work and how to become a clown. They perked up a bit when they started doing their own makeup and learning about how to twist a balloon. But the transformation was obvious and exciting when they worked the room of the elderly adults, chatting, being funny, and

---

[12] Andrea Hirschfeld, a.k.a. All Ears, holds an M.A. in Social Service Administration from the University of Chicago. She has worked as the administrator of the Mitzvah Clowns since 2001, and continues to run workshops throughout the country.

enjoying their own success from behind their masks; not only were they bringing joy to other people, but the project also served to raise the children's self-esteem when they felt the impact of their generous work.

It was at that moment that I understood that the intrinsic re-ward for one *Mitzvah* is another *Mitzvah*. We like to believe that we are simply altruistic when it comes to *Mitzvah* work– we do it because we are commanded to improve the world in some way. The positive feeling we get from the work we do, however, comes back to us in spades. It has truly helped my children, now 15 and 24, understand what makes their lives worth living. One is shy while the other very outgoing and social, and they each have benefited from their *Mitzvah* work in different ways. *Mitzvah* Clowning gave my more reserved daughter the strength to approach people because she recognizes the joy she receives from benefiting others. For the outgoing one, I believe it has helped her understand and appreciate that the world is not as simple and easy to handle for everyone as it is for her. She has gained great insight and a sense of empathy from working to help others, even in the smallest ways, when she performs as a visiting clown.

All of us who call ourselves '*Mitzvah* Clowns' have experienced the joy of service since starting our work. We have experienced joy not only from pastoral visits but also as we each teach others to become a *Mitzvah* clown. And yet, these *Mitzvot* are not ours to own in a single, special way. We do the work, others benefit, and still more people continue to do the work. It is a fulfilling action and clearly shows how one *Mitzvah* leads to the next.

I was raised as a completely unaffiliated Jew. I identified with my Jewish roots as the product of my parents; one who fought in WWII and one who was the victim of anti-Semitism in a much-segregated Chicago during Hitler's reign. I strongly identified with being Jewish, but I had no formal training or study. My children, however, would be raised differently. We joined the local *Shul* (congregation) and dutifully sent our children to Jewish nursery and Hebrew school. It was during this time that I, as well as my children, learned about *Mitzvot*. A *Mitzvah*, as it had been explained, was a commandment we followed like the act of lighting *Shabbat* candles, keeping kosher, keeping *Shabbat*. But it was also doing the simple things that help make our world a better place.

And it was something we could do individually or with a group.

What a concept for me to learn as an adult! Life wasn't about just providing for my family. Working with others for the betterment of the world, without any monetary reward or formal recognition gave me a new perspective on life. *Mitzvah* clowning has allowed me to pass on that perspective without deliberately telling students and my own children that establishing an identity of helping others and working to make the world a better place for no monetary reward is just something *we should do as Jews and as human beings.* When my family sees the joy I get from sharing clowning with them and with others, they can't help but understand how it all works – creating a *Mitzvah*, the rewards for doing a *Mitzvah*, and the ways in which *Mitzvot* come back to us in ways we can't imagine or understand. Though it was through clowning that my children found their voice in *Tikun Olam* and *Bikur Cholim*, I believe they would have found that same voice from any mitzvah-based activity. There is a special level of esteem that comes from community service and helping others. All the praise and love I could have given my children as their parent would not have developed that level of independence and self-esteem for them. It is developed internally and is a direct result of the work they've done to make a most important difference in other's lives.

Chapter 9: Hospitality - *Hachnesat Orchim*
To Care For Others Is To See the Face Of God

Hospitality is greater than a visit to the House of Study.
(Shabbat 127a)

Behavior is a mirror in which everyone shows his
own image. (Goethe)

A Good Person: Yoel Dorkam

As a child, Yoel lived through the *Shoah*, the destruction of the Jews in Europe. In order to survive his family had to leave Nazi Germany by crossing many borders. Yoel spent his thirteenth year in a Spanish prison. Eventually he arrived in Palestine and fought in the War of Independence in 1948. He later settled in *Kibbutz Palmach Tzuba*,[13] outside of Jerusalem.

Besides Yoel's regular jobs at the *kibbutz* (tractor driver, harvester, glass factory employee, etc). he took on a responsibility that has transformed the State of Israel; he was the director of the Ya'akov Maimon Volunteers. Ya'akov Maimon organized Israeli citizens to help new immigrants adjust to their new homeland and learn Hebrew. When he died in 1960 Yoel became the director. He has worked with immigrants from the former Soviet Union, Ethiopia, Iraq, Syria and other places to settle together in their "new" home.

*   *   *

I grew up in a very modest home. When I was a child we joked that our parents protected the living room furniture with plastic covers. My mother spent money (I thought) we could ill afford for two top quality linen sets that she never used until my aunt came to stay the night. I could always tell when guests were coming because there were sheets, silverware and dishes that were only put out for them.

---

[13] This kibbutz was founded by Palmachniks, the strike force of the Haganah, the organization that would become the Israel Defense Forces.

And, of course, the good furniture was encased in plastic. I used to complain that she was saving the best for people who would only stay one night. What about us, the ones that lived there every day?

My mother believed that one of the marks of a good person was how they treated their guests – so it wasn't surprising that she reserved the special things just for them. She was right.

We had many different types of "guests" in our home; some we knew some we didn't. Someone in "need" would become a "guest." Off came the plastic covers and out came the good dishes. I learned a new meaning of the word "*Tzedakah*."

Most people think that the definition of *Tzedakah* is "charity" or "giving money to poor people." That is one form of *Tzedakah* – but not it's definition. *Tzedakah* means "justice," or "the right thing." When we talk about giving or doing *Tzedakah* we are talking about "doing the right thing." There are many ways of doing the right thing, and many things that can be done right. The use of money to help those in need is only one example. There are many others.

There are many *Mitzvot* that qualify as "acts of *Tzedakah*." Hospitality is an appropriate first step. *Bachya ben Asher* reported that there was a custom in Medieval Spain, before the Inquisition, among families of prominence. They would utilize the boards of the dining room table in the construction of the burial casket.

Imagine that. Today we pay thousands of dollars for a casket that is polished, stained wood; a casket that will only be visible for an hour or two at most. But back then, the more the table was used, the greater number of people who had been invited to share a meal with the family, the more scratched, faded, the more used the casket would look.

Imagine if our caskets were not symbols of how much money we wished to spend on someone lost to us forever, but instead, were used to symbolize how loved or revered that person had been in life.

We learn about the *Mitzvah Hachnesat Orchim*, or hospitality, from the *Torah*.

> *God appeared to him (Abraham) at Elonay Mamray. He was sitting at the opening of the tent during the heat of the day. He lifted his eyes to see and there were three men standing over him. He ran from the opening of the tent to greet them. He bowed to the ground. He said, "My lords, if I have found favor in your eyes do not pass before me. Take a little water and wash your feet. Rest here under the tree. I will take a slice of bread and you will refresh yourselves.*
> *(Genesis 18:1-5)*

We learn many lessons from Abraham for he is the Patriarch of the Jewish people. In this text we notice that he didn't wait for the visitors to approach. He went out to greet them. He immediately sets them at ease by bowing. He was not concerned about ego or status. He just wanted to host them. He immediately offers them food and does not give them the opportunity to "politely refuse."

Later on in the text we will find that these strangers are really Divine messengers. They have come to inform Abraham and Sarah of the future birth of their son Isaac and to destroy the cities of *Sodom* and *Gomorrah*. The tradition identifies these two cities as places of ultimate evil. The rabbis ask, "What made these cities so evil," Many of the answers refer to their perversion of *Tzedakah* and hospitality.

In one text about *Sodom* we learn how every stranger asking for money would be given gold pieces by the residents. Each piece would have the name of the person who gave it embossed on the coin. The stranger would amass much gold, but *Sodom's* laws forbade anyone to sell food to him. After he starved to death, each *Sodomite* would come to the body and reclaim their gold coins.

The *Mitzvah* of *Hachnasat Orchim* is also unique in that you must have the proper way and attitude in performing the *Mitzvah*; it cannot be done grudgingly or without intent. You cannot allow your guest to feel uncomfortable or even believe that what you are offering constitutes a sacrifice on your part.

> *Hospitality is more important even than encountering God's intimate presence.*
> (Shabbat 127a)

We learn that giving comfort to those around us is more important than encountering God. Perhaps this is because if we don't comfort those in need around us, we have no chance of ever encountering God. However, this *Mitzvah* need not be done only at home. It does not only consist of opening up one's home to strangers. In a broader sense, it consists of opening one's heart to the needs of others, as well.

Home Work:

1. Find a local chapter of Habitat for Humanity or Christmas in July in your area. Volunteer.
2. Do you know someone in your community who needs hospitality for holiday meals? Do you have room at your holiday table?
3. Find organizations in your area that provide shelter for the homeless. Would you be willing to staff a program in a congregation that houses "guests" between Christmas and New Year, or during the year?

Story:

Once there was a poor but honest man named Eli. He had no money, but he made it his business that no stranger to the town was left without a home to sleep in on Shabbat. One day, Elijah came to the town in the guise of a poor old beggar. Eli shared his meager home with him and they spent a wonderful Shabbat together. When it came time for Elijah to leave he asked Eli "If you could wish for anything, what would you wish for?" Eli replied without hesitation, "Enough money to open an inn for travelers; where I could greet many different people and make sure that all the poor had a roof over their heads every Shabbat."

Elijah blessed Eli and, as time passed, Eli came into some money which he invested in an inn. His hospitality was famous and his name became so well known that people would come from miles around just to spend an evening at his inn.

As his fame grew, there was less and less room for the poor at his inn. Eli did not want to let people who were not dressed properly or who had not bathed in some time under his roof – it might affect the joy of his customers.

Elijah came back to visit Eli, and though he was not dressed that well, Eli recognized him as the man who had blessed him and greeted him with laughter and pride. He asked Elijah to stay for Shabbat but Elijah refused. He pointed to the window and asked Eli,

"What do you see?"

"People of all sorts, but mostly poor people."

Then Elijah showed Eli a mirror and asked:

"What do you see?"

"Only myself."

Elijah continued, "Isn't that interesting, they are both made of glass but one allows you to see others outside and one only allows you to see yourself. The difference between the two is one thin layer of silver. The silver only allows you to see yourself."

Eli immediately understood and opened his doors to the poor.

Chapter 10: Respect For That Which Has Lived – *K'vod Hamet*. Compassion Does Not End When Life Does

He who disbelieves in the performance of kind deeds is a disbeliever in that which is fundamental (the belief in God). (Kohelet Rabbah 7)

In a culture where few are even willing to grow old, it is not surprising that death is sometimes viewed as if it were a social problem. (Rachel Naomi Remen)

A Good Person: Jeannie Jaybush

There is nothing more devastating than the death of an infant. After nine months of pregnancy, hoping and praying for a healthy baby, making plans for its future, losing a baby at birth or soon thereafter is a tragedy from which many parents never fully recover.

Funeral costs only add to the tragedy. Add the cost of the cemetery plot, casket and funeral home services can add an intolerable financial burden to an already emotionally distraught family.

And, if the family is poor – what do they do? How do you preserve any dignity when you can't afford to place a baby at rest in a respectful manner?

Jeannie Jaybush is the director of St. Joseph's Baby Corner in Seattle, Washington. St. Joseph's Baby Corner is an organization that provides the necessities for new parents who don't have the money to provide for their children. They buy and deliver car seats, portable cribs, diapers and everything necessary to raise healthy children.

In 1995, Jeannie encountered a poor family who had lost their baby. They were poor but not poor enough. They fell "between the cracks" of social care agencies. If they had been receiving public assistance, the state would have arranged to have the baby's remains cremated. However, the father worked two jobs to keep the family off public assistance and they didn't want their child cremated. They did not have the money for a burial.

In working with this family Jeannie found out that this was not a unique situation – it happened more often than anyone was comfortable talking about. Jeannie lobbied the Archbishop for them and others who might encounter the same situation.

It took her two years but she was finally successful. The community would now take responsibility to help and support families in similar tragic circumstance.

*   *   *

For the last nine years of her life, my mother lived with us; three generations under one roof. To use one half of Charles Dickens's famous quote, "It was the best of times." She moved in while she was healthy – and we were able to enjoy her health to the extreme. Her death, after long illness, was one of the greatest challenges our family has ever faced. Today, years after the fact, we are still learning from her and learning about ourselves from the experience.

We live in a country where advanced technology has been harnessed to keep us healthy and alive. Never have so many lived so long in productive roles within our society. Proof of this is all around us. Not too many years ago great-grandparents were a rarity. Grandfathers were rarely alive; grandmothers wore black dresses with black stockings and black shoes. They stayed at home and smiled a lot. Today, grandparents are youthful[14] and great-grandparents are not unusual. It is safe to say that almost no one has a grandmother who always wears black and stays at home.

Concurrent with our longer and more active life-spans has been the largely successful attempt to make death and the process of dying something hidden and rarely discussed. Death is no longer seen as a natural part of life; a transition from one world to the next. More than ever, it is the elephant in the room; unnoticed and not discussed.

Jewish tradition teaches that death is a part of life. The two are inseparable. Just as we respect those who are alive and in need during their transition, we are required to honor and respect the remains of

---

[14] I serve as witness to this phenomenon. I became a grandparent only a few years ago and do things with my granddaughter that my grandmothers never dreamed of. I expect to live long enough to see her married, no matter what age she chooses to, whereas both my grandmothers passed away long before my Bar Mitzvah.

those who have lived during the process of funeral and burial.

> *If a person is near death, it is forbidden to leave him, so that he should not die alone. And it is a Mitzvah to stand by a person at the moment of death.*
> *(Shulchan Aruch, Yoreh Deah 339:4)*

If it is a *Mitzvah* to honor someone before they die, how much more should we honor the memory and the body of the person who lived after they die?[15]

To me, this *Mitzvah* is paramount within our tradition. How we treat the memory of our deceased reflects our values and loyalty to tradition. As uncomfortable as this might be, the funeral is the most important life cycle event in the life of a family.[18]

According to the tradition there are two parts to this *Mitzvah*. The funeral is composed of actions and rituals completed out of respect for the deceased, from the time of death until the completion of the funeral at the cemetery, the focus is on the deceased. However, once the burial is over, everything that takes place at the *Shiva*[16] home is done out of respect for the mourners. The goal is to give them the support of all who wish to help while at the same time give them the opportunity to deeply grieve their loss.

Funerals are meant to be simple ceremonies. They are supposed to show respect for the specific individual who has died and, at the same time, treat everyone equally – so that no one is embarrassed by the ceremony. Too often we confuse "honoring the dead" with expensive caskets and elaborate ceremonies. We honor those who have passed

---

[15] This Mitzvah has great meaning to me because of the lessons I learned in seminary. I entered the seminary unsure of my choice. I took a leave of absence after my first year and went home to study for a year. Because I lived in a small southern town which did not have the resources to hire a full time rabbi, I was asked to perform the clergy functions during that year. After I officiated at my first funeral I recognized the importance of the mitzvah and the rabbis who enable it.

[16] *Shiva* refers to the seven days of intense mourning following the loss of an immediate relative.

away by keeping their memory alive, speaking of them and mourning them in appropriate ways.

> *At first, burying the dead was more difficult for the relatives than the death itself, because of the enormous expense. Relatives even abandoned the bodies and ran away. Finally, Rabban Gamliel adopted a simple style and the people adopted a simple style and the people carried him to his grave in linen garments. Subsequently everyone followed his example and carried out the dead in similar fashion, even in cloth that was worth only a zuz (small amount).* (Ketuvot 8b)

We also honor the living who mourn the deceased and provide a respectful way for everyone to show condolence without being humiliated.

> *Formerly it was the custom to bring food to the house of mourning. The rich bringing it in silver and gold baskets, the poor in wicker baskets. The result was that the poor felt embarrassed. They therefore decreed that all should use wicker baskets out of consideration for the poor.* (Moed Katan 27a)

We honor those who have lived before in our preparations for the funeral. A *Chevrah Kadishah* (literally "holy group") prepares the body with ritual washing and dressing. We honor them during the ceremony by speaking to their memory and by observing mourning customs. After the period of *Shivah* we honor them by reciting *Kaddish* at the appropriate times.

It has been said that Judaism is a religion where the generations are in constant dialogue. By learning *Torah* we speak with sages who taught the *Torah* centuries ago. We are in dialogue with those we have never seen and those we will never know. At the core of our tradition is the belief that as long as these conversations continue we will honor all those who have contributed to them and are no longer with us. As long as we remain active in the conversation no one is ever forgotten.

Home Work:

1. We honor the memory of those who have died by bestowing their names upon their children and grandchildren. Who are you named after? Discuss as a family who each member is named after. If you have videos or photographs to illustrate the stories, use them.
2. As a family, look at the obituary page from a local paper. Compare the write-ups. What can you tell about the values of the person who died from what is written in the obituary?
3. If you have relatives there, visit the cemetery. Recite the memorial prayers for those you knew and tell stories of those who are buried there.
4. Contact an elderly member of the congregation and offer as a family to take them to the cemetery to visit their loved ones. Learn how to recite the memorial prayers for them.

Story:

There is a parable about the difference between heaven and hell. In hell people are seated at a table overflowing with delicious food. But they have splints on their elbows and so they cannot reach their mouths with their spoons. They sit through eternity experiencing a terrible hunger in the midst of abundance. In heaven people are also seated at a table overflowing with delicious food. They, too, have splints on their elbows and cannot reach their mouths. But in heaven, people use their spoons to feed one another. Perhaps hell is always of our own making. In the end, the difference between heaven and hell may only be that in hell, people have forgotten how to bless one another...

(Midrash as told by Rachel Naomi Remen)

Chapter 11: Do Not Waste - *Bal Tashchit*
Murder in a Different Form?

God cannot live in the same world with the proud and arrogant man. Let man always learn from the mind of his Creator, who paid no heed to the other high mountains and peaks, but caused His Presence to rest upon Mount Sinai, which is not difficult to ascend... God is exalted, yet He regards the lowly. (Sotah, 5a)

Anything worth doing is worth doing badly.
(C.K. Chesterton)

A Good Person: Ranya Kelly

Meeting Ranya for the first time you would never guess that this quiet petite woman once brought a major corporation to its knees in the city of Denver. She never intended to be a controversial celebrity but, when you get to know her you will find that Ranya never backs away from a fight when she is in the right.

Several years ago she found herself in need of a good sized box to send out a gift. She went in back of a strip mall store that sold shoes to find such a box but, when she opened the dumpster, found 500 pair of brand new shoes instead. The store, and its parent company, had a policy to discard merchandise that did not sell after a certain amount of time.

Ranya took the shoes home and invited her family and friends to take what they wanted. But she still had hundreds of pairs of shoes left – and would not throw them out. She ended up driving to a homeless shelter to donate the shoes. There, she had an epiphany. As she put it, "I never knew about the shelters or people who really needed anything. I grew up in an upper middle class family. I was never involved with poor people. There was a pregnant woman standing in the doorway, her pants dragging on the floor. She had a two or three year old in tow and had no shoes. It was the middle of January. I just couldn't comprehend that somebody didn't have a pair of shoes when I had just found 500 pair."

Ranya went back to that dumpster and began collecting the

discarded shoes. She was caught, almost arrested for theft and almost sued. When they could not stop her the store began shredding the shoes to stop her.

Finally, after the press got involved and both sides began talking, Ranya was allowed to continue. Today, almost one million shoes later, she has created an organization that brings stores which habitually discard unsold merchandise together with people who are in need. Ranya's organization, The Redistribution Center, channels millions of dollars worth of materials every year.

*   *   *

I have known Ranya for more than twenty years and have facilitated redistribution programs in New Jersey, Mississippi, and Kentucky. Opening the trucks and watching our "clients" see what is inside brings tears to our volunteer eyes. I remember one director of a program in Newark, New Jersey blessing us all – reminding us again and again how much life we were spreading around.

I cry. In part I cry because I don't realize how much a brand new pair of jeans means to a Mississippi teen who has to wear torn sweatpants because even now, years after Hurricane Katrina, the family can't afford clothing. I cry because a Kentucky schoolchild will have a new backpack instead of a plastic garbage bag for her school supplies. And I cry because as sensitized as I have become to the needs around us, I still live in an upper/middle class community known for its wealth and high educational standards. I remember quite clearly years ago, the response when I approached a local minister to co-sponsor Ranya Kelly's Redistribution Center, where we would be able to bring thousands of dollars of new clothing and household goods for those in need. He said, "There are no poor people in our town."

And he was right. To the superficial observer there were no poor in our town. He was surprised when I told him I had just paid for a new furnace for one of my congregants who, with winter approaching, could not afford to repair their old furnace. To him, something must be wrong with them if they were in need.

I learned about this *Mitzvah* at an early age. It was not my best day in *Yeshiva*. I hated milk, and I had to drink my carton of milk every day at lunch. But, one day God was with me. The carton of milk I picked up was empty – an accident for some, but a miracle for me. What do you do with an empty yet sealed milk carton? My classmate Joey came up with a novel idea. He threw it at the 8th grade table. They threw it back. This was great fun for we (the 7th graders) had finally gotten the 8th grade to notice us. Eventually, Jay (an 8th grader) got tired of this and threw an apple back. Things began to get out of hand until Roy. whose lunch had been smashed by bits of apple, came over and beat up Joey.[17]

The rabbis pieced these events together and conferred as to what punishments should be meted out. Roy was suspended for a week from school – he beat up a kid. Joey was let off (he had suffered enough). Jay was also suspended for two days. Why? He had wasted food.

That was how I learned the *Mitzvah* of *Bal Tashchit*.

We begin with a text:

> *Whoever breaks vessels, or tears garments or destroys a building or clogs a well, or does away with food in a destructive manner violates the negative Mitzvah of Bal Tashchit.*
> *(Kiddushin 32a)*

There is an important lesson to be learned from this text. We usually think of *Bal Tashchit* as a refusal to recycle or throwing out leftovers from a *Simcha or Kiddush*. While it is true that these actions are embodiments of *Bal Tashchit*, they are not the only examples. Anyone who acts in a manner destructive to the community welfare also violates this law. Anyone who could have done something productive and refuses, or turns away violates this law. Anyone who shows contempt for others and their needs violates this law.

Maimonides, in his commentary adds more categories:

---

[17] A cautionary note; the names have been changed to protect the guilty.

> *The Law forbids only wanton destruction...Not only one who cuts down trees, but also one who smashes household goods, tears clothing, demolishes a building, stops up a spring, or destroy articles of food with destructive intent, transgresses the command of "Bal Tashchit." (Mishneh Torah: Kings & Wars 6:8-10)*

To waste is to actively squander gifts given to us by God. We have been blessed with the ability to create wondrous things. Allowing them to go to waste shows a lack of respect for the creations and their Creator.

> *The purpose of this Mitzvah is to teach us to love that which is good and worthwhile and to cling to it, so that good becomes a part of us...This is the way of the righteous and those who improve society, who love peace and rejoice in the good in people and bring them close to Torah: That nothing, not even a grain of mustard, should be lost to the world, that they should regret any loss or destruction that they can.*
> *(Sefer Hachinuch #529)*

Home Work:

1. Conduct a personal *Bal Tashchit* campaign before birthdays and Chanukah.
2. Collect used books for donation to local reading programs.
3. Ask to set up a special *Bal Tashchit* corner on your congregation's website: list what things people have that they no longer need. Match needs to items available.
4. Do a "family dumpster dip" of local businesses. Be sure to wear rubber gloves. Take note of what is thrown away. Be a matchmaker! Contact local shelters to see if they can use the refuse of these businesses. Contact the businesses to see if they will donate the "garbage" to the shelters.

5. Take a personal inventory of all the "trash" you create in one day. How much can be "saved?"
6. Brainstorm with the family as to what items (eyeglasses, hearing aids, etc.) could be collected for donations to local programs and how to do so.

Story:

Rabbi Shlomo and his student Rabbi Mordechai of Lechovitz once traveled cross country. It was toward the end of the period in which the blessing of the New Moon can be spoken. Since the shining sickle had broken from the clouds which had been veiling it, they appeared for the sacred rite. But, the coachman anticipated them. The moment he saw the new moon, he wiped his hands and mumbled the blessing. Rabbi Mordechai laughed, but his teacher reproved him.

"A king once gave an order to collect all the leftovers of the meal eaten in his army and store them in a certain place. No one knew the reason for the command. But presently the country was at war. The king's army was surrounded by the enemy and cut off from outside provisions. Then the king fed his army on the leftovers, which the enemy laughingly let pass. The army kept up its strength and was victorious.

(Buber: Tales of the Hasidim, p. 279)

Chapter 12: Guarding the Earth/Ecology - *Shomrei Adamah*
The Earth is Ours and the Glory Thereof

*If you have a seedling in your hand and are on the point of
planting it and someone comes to tell you that the
Messiah has arrived, finish your planting first (and then
go to greet her). (Avot D'Rabbi Natan 31)*

*The future depends on what we do in the present.
(Mahatma Gandhi)*

A Good Person: Andy Lipkis

One day as a camper in a summer camp near his home in Los Angeles, Andy Lipkis' counselor showed him a hillside of trees turning brown in the middle of summer. "In 25 years those hills will be completely brown. There won't be any trees at all." Smog from the city was killing the trees.

At the age of 15 Andy began a campaign to save the trees. He found types of trees that were not affected by smog and began planting them. By the time he was 18, Andy had 20 camps working with him. Through hard work and perseverance Andy got 8,000 smog resistant saplings from the State of California for free. A freshman in college at the time, Andy had to accept delivery of the saplings at his college dorm. With help from the cafeteria manager and an ice cream store owner, Andy was able to keep the saplings refrigerated until he could find 8,000 empty milk cartons from a dairy company and find the dozens of students needed to transport and transplant the trees in the hills.

Andy and his helpers were dubbed "the tree people" and the name stuck. Treepeople work to plant millions of trees all over the world.

*   *   *

When I was growing up everyone always talked about a "generation gap;" that there was a disconnect between the values of my parents and myself. Ecology seems to be one of those issues that highlights a modern generation gap. I was not brought up to be concerned about the earth, my children have taught me. This is significant because this *Mitzvah* is unique as an example of how children can teach their parents. My children taught me the value of *Shmirat Adamah*, Guarding the Earth, not the other way around.

In family educational dynamics it is important that the information and lessons flow in both directions. This makes the family a team that works together.

Did you know that the average person in the United States produces four pounds of "garbage" a day? Did you know that recycling the paper from one Sunday edition of the New York Times could save 75,000 trees?

Some six-packs of soda are held together in plastic loops. If you throw the plastic loops into the garbage, many of the loops will end up in the ocean or in landfills. Garbage attracts animals that feed off the waste. Some of the scavengers, like seagulls, have long beaks which fit quite snugly into the plastic loops. Birds and fish do not have hands to remove the plastic from their beaks or mouths. The result? They starve to death.

The easiest way to avoid murdering animals in this way is to recycle all plastic. However, if you belong to a community that does not recycle, just take a scissors and cut the plastic loops into shreds. You will render the plastic harmless to animal life. If you don't recycle or cut the loops, you are committing murder. Before you read this paragraph it was accidental. Now that you know – you have a responsibility to prevent it.

We are all familiar (as either children or parents) with the eternal cry, "Clean up your room?" I sometimes feel that God is repeating that phrase as a mantra, over and over again. The consequences of humanity refusing to clean up its room will be the death and extinction of many species of animals. This is not a task we can hire others to do – cleaning "our" room is *our* responsibility.

> *In the hour when the Holy One created the first human being, God took the person before all the trees of the Garden of Eden and said to the person, "See my works, how fine and excellent they are! Now all that I have created, for you have I created. Think upon this, and do not corrupt and desolate my world. For if you corrupt it, there is no one to set it right after you."* (Kohelet Rabbah 7:28)

As crazy as it might seem, there are those who believe that Jewish tradition is unconcerned with ecology. They preach that "Man" is the acme of Creation and all creatures were created to serve humankind. Thus, anything that we do, whether it causes the extinction of a species or not is fine – for the "caretaker of Creation" has complete discretionary powers. They point to the lack of ecological concern in the *Torah* and use that as proof that this is not a *Mitzvah*.

We must remember that our ancestors lived at a time when there was no concept of endangered resources. The depletion of one area was not cause for concern. But they were commanded to keep all fields fallow every seventh year, demanding *Shabbat* rest.

> *It should not be believed that all the beings exist for the sake of the existence of humanity. On the contrary, all other beings too have been intended for their own sakes, and not for the sake of something else.*
> (Maimonides, Guide for the Perplexed 456)

Every being is part of God's plan. More to the point, we must recognize that we too occupy a niche along with every other species in Creation. We may be central to God's purpose, but the depth and complexity of Creation does not allow us to arbitrarily manipulate other's creations to our whim. Indeed, there are lessons and values we can learn from other species.

> *But ask the beasts, and they will teach you: the birds of the sky and they will tell you. Or speak to the earth and it will teach you, the fish or the seal, they will inform you. Who among all these does not know that the hand of the Eternal has done this?* (Job 12:7 - 9)

There are lessons and values we can learn from other species. Ask anyone who has ever owned a pet and they will tell you how important knowing an animal can be. Nursing homes that allow pets find that it is a significant factor in lengthening the lives of its residents and lessening their medication.[18]

In addition to the killing of species, the murder of animals and plants and the destruction of eco-systems is an insult to God. In essence, we have taken God's creation, given to us for safekeeping, and defiled it. How can we ask God to be cognizant of our needs when we are so cavalier with God's possessions?

We are gifted with intelligence. We are blessed with the insight to understand what will happen if we do not conserve. Allowing destruction without complaint is a violation of the *Mitzvah* "Do Not Stand Idly By." *Shmirat Adamah* is closely related to this. "*Al Ta'amod*" (Do not stand idly by) while the earth is being destroyed.

> *One day Choni the circle drawer was journeying on the road and he saw a man planting a carob tree. He asked him, "How long does it take for this tree to bear fruit?" The man replied, "Seventy years." Choni then further asked him, "Are you certain that you will live another seventy years?" The man replied, "I found ready grown carob trees in the world, as my ancestors planted these for me, so I too plant these for my children."* (Ta'anit 23a)

---

[18] I wrote about Dr. William Thomas and his Eden Alternative in chapter 8.

The rest of the story is instructive. *Choni*[19] scoffs at the man and his planting. God causes *Choni* to fall into a deep sleep.[20] *Choni* awakens to see the carob tree has blossomed and the man's grandchildren enjoying the fruit of the carob. *Choni* finds that his name has all but been forgotten in the world and that those who know of him speak as though he has been gone for a thousand years. In the end, he asks God for death, to ease his misery.

This story is very poignant and contains many different messages. Primary among them though, is that our legacy can be found in how we plan for our children. *Choni* was revered as a great teacher but he left no material legacy. The carob tree is a constant reminder of its planter and his contributions to his grandchildren's welfare. If we want to leave something tangible for our grandchildren, something that will make them remember us with blessing – plant a carob tree.

Today things are not so different. My mother saved her money so that her grandchildren could experience Israel in a way that she never could. She wanted them to have tangible benefits from her experience and her legacy. I save so that my children will not have to start with as little as I did. I hope this value will be passed down to my children.

Why can't we do the same thing with our planet? Why can't we see our environment as a natural resource that is also a gift from God? Why can't we see it as a resource that we will bequeath to our grandchildren? If we recycled with the same fervor that we invest in stocks or mutual funds, we would be much better off.

Home Work:

1. Collect articles from local papers and magazines about conservation. Discuss the articles. What Jewish values can you find in these articles?
2. Visit a local recycling center. Learn what items can be recycled.

---

[19] According to Rabbinic legend, *Choni Hama'agal, Choni* the circle drawer got his name because during a severe drought he drew a circle around himself and refused to leave it until God sent rain. When the rains came *Choni*'s name was legend.

[20] Which is why *Choni* is called the "Jewish Rip Van Winkle," although it seems to me that Rip is really the Dutch *Choni*.

3. Plant a vegetable garden. Donate the produce to a local soup kitchen. You can use www.ampleharvest.org as a resource.
4. Do a home survey of cleaning products that are hazardous to the environment. Take a trip to the supermarket to identify products that are <u>not</u> hazardous to the environment.

Story:

When Noah came out of the ark, he opened his eyes and saw the whole world completely destroyed.

He began crying for the world and said, God, how could you have done this?

God replied, "Oh Noah. when I told you I would destroy the entire world, I lingered and delayed, so that you would speak on its behalf. But when you knew you would be safe in the ark, you were content. You thought of no one but you and your family. And now you complain?" Then Noah knew that he had sinned.

(Midrash Tankhuma, Parashat Noach)

Chapter 13: Do Not Stand Idly By - *Al Ta'amod*
We Are Our Brother's Keeper

*If a person closes his eyes to avoid giving any charity,
it is as if he committed idolatry. (Ketuvot 68a)*

*I've been able to overcome my fears because of an acute sense
of an even greater fear – that of feeling remorse. You can
live with pain. You can live with embarrassment. Remorse
is an awful companion. Whatever the unwelcome
consequences of courage, they are unlikely to be worse
than the discovery that you are less than you
pretend to be. (John McCain)*

A Good Person: Jay Feinberg

In June of 1991, Jay Feinberg, a "typical" 23 year old, graduated from college. But Jay's world collapsed when he was diagnosed with CML Chronic Myelogenous Leukemia. His only hope was a bone marrow transplant. Ironically, Jay's two brothers matched each other, but neither matched Jay.

In September of 1991, Jay's parents, unable to find a donor, founded an organization called "Gift of Life" to encourage people to get their blood typed in the hope that one of the many thousands tested would match Jay. Never did they imagine, when they started, how far and how wide their efforts would go. "Gift of Life" has been responsible for hundreds of drives held all over the world, even in Byelorussia, where many of Jay's relatives lived.

The Feinbergs, in their effort to find a "match" for Jay, raised millions of dollars, "typed" thousands and thousands of Jews all over the globe and raised awareness in the Jewish community of the critical nature that every individual be tested. More importantly, many other leukemia patients in need of a transplant also found matches.

It took several years, but finally, in July of 1995, a match was found for Jay. Today, many years later Jay is living life and in the process helping many others as they seek their match.

* * *

To me, this *Mitzvah* is one of the hardest to define and observe because it takes so many forms and is present in so many situations. In third grade my daughter found a best friend because she refused to stand idly by while she was being bullied by a group of girls. We helped pay the college tuition of another daughter's friend who had run out of funds. The list can be endless because there is always someone who needs help.

It is also a *Mitzvah* that must be learned and modeled at home. I learned this *Mitzvah* from my parents; who were never afraid to incur the wrath of an employer, friends or the community to stand up for someone else who was at risk. I believe that the *Mitzvah* of *Al Ta'amod* is of utmost importance because it attempts to clarify the ethic of our life's involvement.

> *One shall not stand by idly when his brother's blood is being shed.*
> *Leviticus 19:16*

In 1985, the Social Action Committee of the Rabbinical Assembly asked its members living in the Washington D.C area to emulate the protestors at the South African embassy and demonstrate for the freedom of Soviet Jews outside the Soviet embassy. There is a little known law in D.C. which prohibits demonstrating within 500 feet of any embassy.[21] The South African demonstrators were being detained and released. The 24 rabbis and one Lutheran minister who demonstrated in front of the Soviet embassy were arrested and tried.

At the trial we were found guilty and sentenced to 15 days suspended sentence, $50 fine and 6 months probation. At that point we had a decision to make. We had embarked upon this course of action in order to bring attention to the plight of the Soviet Jews. If we refused to pay the fine we would be sentenced to prison, and would bring even more attention to the cause. Five of us decided to refuse the fine – much to the consternation of selected local Jewish leadership and our

---

[21] In a supreme touch of irony, this law was enacted to protect the Nazi German Embassy from protestors in the 1930's.

colleagues. We reasoned that with this unique opportunity before us we could not "stand idly by."

A basic concept within Jewish law is that of collective responsibility, or the responsibility of one individual for the welfare of another. We have only to look at the Holocaust to understand the importance of this *Mitzvah*.

But how far does this mandate go? How pervasive should it be? Are there situations in which we have a choice about whether or not we should get involved? What actions must we take, and under what circumstances? These are the questions we explore throughout our entire lives, hopefully coming up with a consistent set of answers to guide us.

The *Talmud* provides us with examples to model:

> *Avner, the general of King Saul, was punished for not protesting King Saul's actions.*
> (Sanhedrin 20a)

King Saul, the first king of Israel, was a failure as a king. Reading the books of First and Second Samuel, we find that Saul never had "what it took" to succeed. There are many interpretations as to why this happened, but the bottom line is that it did happen.

David, the hero of Israel, was Saul's main competition for the hearts of the Israelites. It became clear to everyone, including Saul, that David would eventually usurp the throne. Saul's response to this threat was to plot David's murder and murder anyone who supported David; introducing a reign of terror destined to bring about his own downfall. Avner, Saul's chief of staff, never protested. Avner is the model of the good officer who was just "following orders." Our tradition teaches that an individual may not abdicate his personal responsibility or judgment. With greater power comes greater obligation and responsibility.

One reason that Avner is such a good example is because the situation is so clear. Avner was Saul's chief of staff. He had only to protest to stop the madness. He provides a clear example to learn from. Life presents us with situations that are not always clear. *Al Ta'amod* directs us to what is always right

In a way, the *Mitzvah* of *Tzedakah* is nothing more than this *Mitzvah* taken to its logical conclusion. We are not allowed to stand by while someone goes in harm's way. Therefore we are required to supply the funds needed to make sure they are never "at risk."

Home Work:

1. Watch the film, *Judgment at Nuremberg* (the Spencer Tracy version). Discuss the reasons given by different German defendants as to why they did "stand idly by."
2. Watch the movie, *Weapons of the Spirit*, about a group of villages in France that harbored over 5,000 Jews during the Holocaust. Discuss and contrast with the above movie.
3. Watch the film, *Joseph Shultz*, a true story about a German soldier who refused to carry out orders of extermination while fighting on the Eastern Front during World War II.
4. Have you been tested to see if you can be a blood marrow donor? How does this action fulfill the *Mitzvah* of "do not stand idly by?"

Story:

One day as Bar Kappara was walking along the shore in Caesarea he saw a ship sinking. One person began to swim ashore but was having trouble. Bar Kappara swam out to save him. At the risk of his own life he brought him to safety. After, Bar Kappara took the man to his home, clothed him, fed him and gave him five dinarim because all his possessions had gone down with the ship.

Months later, it happened that the Jews of Caesarea were imprisoned and threatened with expulsion from the town. Bar Kappara was sent to plead for them, and he was given five hundred dinariim to bribe the judge for a favorable verdict, for such was the way of the Roman courts.

As Bar Kappara pled his case, he handed over the bag of money. To his surprise the judge took out five dinariim and returned the rest.

The judge said, "With five dinariim you saved me, now with five dinariim you have saved your people." (Kohelet Rabbah)

Chapter 14: Ransoming the Captive - *Pidyon Shevuyim*
Half a World Away Is Still Next Door

All Israelites are responsible for each other. (Shevuot 39)

*If there is a terror about darkness because we cannot see,
there is also a terror about light because we can see.
There is a terror about light because much of what we see
in the light about ourselves and our world we would
rather not see, would rather not have seen. (Scott Peck)*

Good People: The Broad Meadows Kids

The 7th graders at Broad Meadows Middle School in Quincy, Massachusetts, had an odd-looking visitor from Pakistan. They knew a child their own age shouldn't look like this boy. Iqbal Masih was so small that his feet didn't reach the floor when he sat in their chairs. And his tiny hands were as rough as an old man's.

Iqbal had been sold into slavery when he was four years old. His family had owed a money lender $12 and the only way they could see to pay the debt was to sell Iqbal.

His "owner" had a carpet factory where Iqbal was taught to make carpets. He was chained to the carpet loom 14 hours a day. He was fed little and beaten often. For six years he dreamed of being free and going to school. When he was ten, he heard a speech by a man from an organization that was trying to stop slavery in Pakistan. This began a long process which ended in Iqbal's freedom. The organization arranged for Iqbal to leave his village and attend school.

Iqbal wasn't satisfied with just being free. He became an activist; giving speeches against child slavery and leading protests in front of factories where children were slaves. Now, he had come to the United States to accept an award for his bravery.

The kids at Broad Meadows were amazed by Iqbal's story, especially when he told them that there were more than seven million slave children in his country. They promised to help, even though they weren't sure what they could do.

Iqbal went back to Pakistan. Just a few months after he visited

Broad Meadows, he was assassinated. He had told the Broad Meadows students that it was dangerous to speak out against child slavery, but they hadn't realized how dangerous.

The class decided to build a school in Iqbal's village, in his memory. They were determined to raise the money in just one year. They planned their campaign. The theme was, "A Bullet Can't Kill a Dream. Help Keep Iqbal's Dream Alive." They used a school computer to email other schools, asking each school to donate $12. They chose that number because Iqbal was sold for $12 and he was 12 years old when he died. They also wrote letters to newspapers and businesses, telling people about Iqbal's life and asking them to help. They called carpet stores to tell them that some Pakistani carpets are made by enslaved children.

At the end of the year the kids had $100,100. They began searching for a principal and teachers to hire. They have bought back dozens of children from slavery. They continue helping children around the world.

*   *   *

Perhaps the greatest act of *Tzedakah* I ever witnessed[22] came during my third year in the pulpit rabbinate. I was serving a congregation in suburban D.C. when Operation Solomon began; the first organized large scale exodus of Jews from Ethiopia. Jewish communities around the world had to raise millions of dollars to make it possible.

The D.C. Jewish community took a very pragmatic approach to their responsibility. They called a meeting of all the congregations and organizations and assigned a dollar amount to each one. Our congregation was told to raise $9,000. This figure was more than $2,000 greater than our best High Holy Day appeal.

We began in the usual ways. Somehow though, this appeal was different. As the stories of the plight of Ethiopian Jewry filtered down to us, we realized that every delay cost the lives of our kin. For some it was the first time they were called to stand up for what they believed in. For

---

[22] What follows was originally published by the Good People Fund on their website under "Voices of Good People."

many in the congregation it was their first chance to save the life of a fellow Jew.

David walked into my office. I had known him for two years. He was in his late twenties, worked at a menial government job and lived alone; a lost soul. David's story was not a happy one. He was abused as a child and afflicted with an emotional illness called "borderline personality disorder." He barely made ends meet. In a good month he lived on soup and crackers the last week. In a bad month I gave him $20 for the soup and crackers.

David walked into my office and gave me five twenty dollar bills for Operation Solomon. I refused. I told him that he was not allowed to starve himself for this project. His response to me has stayed with me to this day. He told me that it was not right for me to refuse the money. "You told me this could save a life." He said, "You can't stop me from doing this. I am finally thinking of someone else. I am finally able to help someone else who has even less than me." I think David saved two lives that day; an Ethiopian Jew he will never know and himself.

There is a story of a great rabbi who asked Elijah where his place in the afterlife would be. Elijah showed him who would be standing with him - a man nobody knew or had ever heard of, but who at one time ransomed captives[23] and brought them to Israel. David could have been that man. I have seen people give hundreds of thousands of dollars for worthy causes, but how many times have they given up their food money to save a life?

David was and forever will be a Good Person.

> *The duty of ransoming captives supersedes the duty of Tzedakah to the poor.*
> *(Maimonides: Mattenot Aniyyim 8:10)*
>
> *Money set aside for charity purposes or for the building of a synagogue may be used to ransom captives.*
> *(Bava Batra 88b)*

---

[23] In the Middle Ages it was common practice for pirates to take Jewish captives and contact the nearest Jewish community for ransom.

This *Mitzvah* has been a Jewish value since the book of Genesis. Avraham[24] raced to save his nephew Lot when Lot was taken captive in war.

> *When Avram heard that his kinsman Lot had been taken captive, he led forth all those who had been born in his household and educated by him, 318 men, and pursued (them) as far as Dan.* (Genesis 14:14)

The irony of the text is that Avraham and Lot were not on speaking terms. Previously they had gone down to Egypt, earning great wealth there. The wealth came between them and their herds-men were in constant conflict. Avraham gave Lot a choice of direction and he went the opposite way. A mark of Lot's new materialistic values is seen in his choice to settle in Sodom. Lot is subsequently taken prisoner when Sodom is conquered.

Yet Avraham did not stop to think about their differences. He did not ask whether Lot would have done the same for him. Lot was a kinsman.

It is a core value of our tradition that we free our captive kinsman whether we know them or not. Traditionally this has been done with almost any means at our disposal; political influence, bribery and force of arms.

---

[24] You will note that the text refers to him as "Avram" while I refer to him as "Avraham." According to the Midrash, a mark of his becoming a Jew was the change of his name from "Avram" to "Avraham." According to Jewish law, one may not refer to him as "Avram" because it is considered unethical to refer to a convert's previous life.

> So Rabbi Meir took a tarkav (measure) full of denarim and set out (to release the sister of his wife from Roman captivity)...He then went to her warden and said, "Hand her over to me." He (the warden) replied, "I am afraid of the government."
> "Take the tarkav of denars, one half distribute (as a bribe), the other half shall be for yourself."
> (Avodah Zarah 18a-b)

Since the Holocaust, the Jewish community has performed this *Mitzvah* by saving the Jews of many countries. Heroic efforts were made before the Holocaust to save the youth of Germany. Jews from the Soviet Union, Ethiopia, Syria and Yemen have all benefited from this *Mitzvah*. We may not know their names or understand their language. Yet, if they are Jews, we are required to help them.

That does not mean we always act in a timely fashion or even with a united effort. But – we do act!!

Home Work:

1. Watch the newspapers for stories about oppressed people around the world. Discuss what is being done to help them? What could you do to help?
2. Read and discuss books and articles about the Holocaust (with older children). Discuss what was and what was not done to help the Jews in Europe.
3. Do an internet search about waves of Israeli immigration; Operation Magic Carpet, Operation Solomon and the like.
4. Contact your local Jewish Community. Borrow DVDs made for Operation Exodus and Operation Solomon. Screen them and discuss.

Story:

Rabbi Shimon bar Yochai prayed that he might behold his neighbor in paradise, and was informed in a dream that it would be a certain butcher whose name and house were also given to him. The Rabbi went to see the butcher and found him to be a wealthy and charitable man.

He said to him, "Please tell me what good deeds you have performed."

The butcher told him that he gave out meat to the poor without charge. This did not satisfy the Rabbi.

He persisted, "Tell me of some unusual deed of goodness you performed."

"Well, I am the collector of the customs at the port. Once the captain of an arriving ship declared to me, 'I have a secret treasure on my vessel. Buy it from me for ten thousand gold pieces, sight unseen. If you do not make the purchase, you will regret it.'

I gave him the money and he delivered to me two hundred Jewish prisoners, men and women. I welcomed them, clothed them, gave them shelter and later presented them with dowries for marriage."

Rabbi Shimon, on hearing this tale, exclaimed, "Praised be the Lord who felt I was worthy to be your neighbor in Paradise."

(Introduction to Midrash Tanchuma, Buber 135)

Chapter 15: Respect For All Human Life - *Mishaneh Habriyot*

Our Rabbis taught, Gemilut Chesed (loving-kindness) is greater than Tzedakah in three ways. Tzedakah is done with one's money, while loving-kindness may be done with one's money or with one's person (spending time with a sick person). Tzedakah is given only to the poor, while loving-kindness may be given both to the poor and to the rich. Tzedakah is given only to the living, while loving–kindness may be shown to both the living and the dead. (Sukkot 49b)

When people are blessed they discover that their lives matter, that there is something in them worthy of blessing and when you bless others, you may discover this same thing is true about yourself. (Rachel Naomi Remen)

Good Person: Hadassah Levi

Hadassah Levi, of Jerusalem, raised more than forty-eight children with Down Syndrome. In 1974, Hadassah was running a day care center for children with mental retardation. She became seriously ill, and, during her stay in a local hospital, noticed that the children with Down Syndrome were being neglected; some were being left near open windows so that they would get sick and die, some were being abandoned by their birth families. Hadassah made a solemn vow that if she were to recover from her illness, she would raise these children. That is how Hadassah Levi opened *"Ma'on Latinok"* (Hebrew, for "a home for infants").

Hadassah destroyed many myths about Down Syndrome as she raised these children. Her children didn't die young because she provided them with a proper environment and medical treatment that some deny these special cases. Above all else, she offered them love.

She fought prejudice from her neighbors who didn't want her there. They were afraid for their children's safety or their property values. They could not stop her.

*   *   *

The Developmentally Disabled:

After I decided to enter the Rabbinate, I applied to the Jewish Theological Seminary (JTS), the Rabbinical school of the Conservative movement. They felt I didn't have enough experience in the Conservative movement. I had gone to Yeshiva for elementary school (an Orthodox environment) and my parents had moved us to a small Southern town when I was in my teens, that supported a small Reform congregation with only a part time Rabbinical student twice a month. They gave me a choice; spend the summer at the JTS taking courses or working at Camp *Ramah*, the camps of the Conservative movement.

Not having the money to become a student, I opted for camp. That summer was the worst summer of my life. I had been brought up at Boy Scout camps, used to camping and outdoor skills. Nothing prepared me for a camp with permanent bunks and the culture shock of campers who did not buy into a strict authority structure.

That summer though, I learned a lot and I began to understand what education truly is. I noticed that there was a set of bunks with special needs campers and that the staff and campers were unique. I decided that if I returned I would only do so as a staff member of the *Tikvah*[25] program.

The next three summers in the *Tikvah* program were close to the best of my life. I learned more about life, people and most of all spirituality from my campers. I learned that when (not if) our community dismisses the various special needs groups that they also dismiss their potential to learn and educate. I learned about God from Jonathan, who on Shabbat morning told our group that he often asked God the question why was he created with Down Syndrome, that God always answered him and that Jonathan was devoting his life to learning how to interpret the answers he received.

When the Rabbis were asked, "What was that most important concept in the *Torah*?" some responded, "People are all created in God's image." Our tradition teaches that everyone is created with the Divine

---

[25] The *Tikvah* program is a program for special needs campers at Camps *Ramah*, the camps of the Conservative movement.

Spark within them. Everyone.

Judaism has a blessing for everything. There is a blessing for when you see a king or queen, when you hear thunder, when you smell a beautiful flower, etc. The concept of "blessing" is simple; by reciting it we recognize God's handiwork and purpose in everything we see or experience. Sometimes that blessing is not easy to say.

There is a blessing that is said whenever you see someone who is physically or mentally different from the "norm." Upon seeing them one says:

Baruch Atta Ado(nai) Elo(h)einu Melech Ha'olam Mishaney Habriyot

*Blessed are You, Lord our God, Sovereign of the Universe,
who formed many varieties of people.*

The literal meaning of the blessing is that when we see someone different, someone "challenged," we still affirm that there is a purpose for that person's life. We recognize this as fact. This is a very emotionally charged issue. Why should we bless God for making people different? Why should we bless God for making some people developmentally disabled?

> *I bless God every day. I pray that I be able to do the best I am able, every day.   (Jonathan)*

A question: I invariably ask classes when I teach this *Mitzvah* is, "Do any of you know a family that has children with developmental disabilities?" Most of the children say "no." Yet I know from experience that this is untrue. The children are not lying: it's just that families with developmentally disabled children tend to stay on the periphery of the Jewish community.

And why shouldn't they? Why should they come into the community? They are rarely welcome. When their children walk into the sanctuary or school we see them as challenges and do not greet them with the warmth and friendliness offered other families. If their child cries out or loses attention during a service, they are ostracized. How many people befriend them?

Several years ago our congregation decided that we needed a dedicated staff person to work with these families – someone who was a trained special educator to help our educational staff and our congregants become more sensitive: someone who would be their advocate. We started a monthly service for children and young adults on the autism spectrum. One of the participants blows the *shofar* for our main service on *Rosh Hashanah*. We bring in tutors for *Bnai Mitzvah* tutoring. We contacted a local organization that works with developmentally disabled adults to bring them into our services and give them membership so that they would feel part of a community. And still we don't do enough.

Chances are you know a family with a developmentally disabled member. Chances are they are not active in the Jewish community. We have the ability to include them. Why we continue to fail in this area is a constant question that needs to be answered.

> The worst problems I ever had were not because of my disabilities. They were from other people dealing with my disabilities.   (Howard)

Howard, may he rest in peace, was another camper of mine at the *Tikvah* program. He was a philosopher. He could find more ways to avoid going swimming than anyone else in the world. He could pun on a dime. He was my camper and he was my teacher. Working with Howard and his friends changed my life. It gave me perspective. It brought me into contact with some of the bravest people I have ever met. It gave me insight into true spirituality.

In writing the *Ziv*/Giraffe curriculum,[26] I was allowed to interview Emily, the daughter of friends and a camper at the *Tikvah* program. Read what she has to teach us about life:

---

[26] The Ziv/Giraffe Curriculum was produced through a donation from the Righteous Person's Foundation. It forms the foundation of this book.

AND YOU SHALL TEACH THEM DILIGENTLY TO YOUR CHILDREN...

> *I go to the Tikvah program at Camp Ramah to learn about my Judaism. Camp is helping me to be more independent. They teach me to do my own laundry at home. They have two separate baskets, lights and darks...I came to camp because it helps me with my handicap.*
>
> *My favorite Mitzvah is "respecting my mom and dad." Also, that there is one God, and you should not bow to other gods. God respects you. Anytime I do something bad, God forgives me. I go to Temple every weekend. I sit with mom except once a month when I help out with a young service called "Tot Shabbat." They treat me like everyone else. I lead Mincha and Ma'ariv at least once a week. We flip a coin to see who will lead.*
>
> *I love my home. Where I used to live, people called me nasty names. It made me upset and mad. I was too slow to walk up the stairs and people would push past me. That never happens at Ramah. Everyone is nice. When other campers in the Tikvah program are sad, I cheer them up by giving them hugs.*
>
> *If I could give God some advice, I would tell Him not to make it rain as often as it does. I don't like rain at camp.*

Did you notice that Emily can lead services? She has hopes and goals like anyone else. She knows that she is different, but she does not let that "difference" prevent her from attaining what she wants. She also has a strong relationship with God. Her belief in God shows a thoughtful theology, especially for a child who is "different."

Emily is quite aware of how people treat her. She didn't like her other school because people were impatient with her. They did not look beyond the stereotype of someone who can't walk, talk, or think fast. She is capable of warmth and recognizes that others need help and support.

Without exception, after almost thirty years in the Rabbinate, two of the most meaningful spiritual and blessed events I ever participated in involved the *Bnai Mitzvah* of developmentally disabled students. And yet we rarely find advocates for these children and adults outside their own family. We will tolerate adults talking during services and we love babies even when they cry – but we castigate the families whose children respond to stimuli we cannot perceive.

The Physically Challenged:

> *Once the blind Rabbi Sheshet was in the synagogue when the Shekhina appeared. The blind and weak Rabbi could not depart from the house quickly enough to satisfy the angels who tormented him. He cried out "O Lord of the universe. I am so weak and You are so mighty, who of us should yield?" A voice was heard, "Leave him in peace."* (Megillah 29)

Even God respects those with physical impairments.

As Jews we try to be inclusive. We spend millions of dollars on outreach programs to keep those on the periphery through choice or circumstance from drifting completely away. Yet we spend almost no money on a group of Jews who are forced to pray in synagogues separate from all others, not because of belief or observance but simply because of their disability.

The deaf Jewish community cannot pray with the hearing Jewish community. Think of what it would take for a deaf Jew to pray in our sanctuaries:
1. A sign language interpreter
2. Reserved seating so that they would have a clear line of sight to the interpreter
3. A special prayer book for them, they can't do responsive readings
4. At least another interpreter so that the deaf Jews could socialize after services
5. Special phone system to communicate with them
6. Different dues structure as, because of their disability they tend to have a lower socio-economic status than the hearing community

Every congregation has a *"bimah".*[27] Being given a *bimah* honor, whether it is opening the ark on the High Holy Days or being asked to come up to bless the *Torah* on Shabbat or holidays is a much sought after honor in most congregations. How would someone in a wheelchair access the *bimah*? Do you have a ramp?

What if you had a parent or grandparent who was confined to a wheelchair and you wanted them to have an honor at the *Bar/Bat Mitzvah* of your child? What if the only way they could take the Aliyah was to be physically carried up the stairs? What would you do?

What if you were the grandparent? Would you take the *Aliyah*? How would you feel if you knew that when you joined a congregation you would never be offered an honor?

> *A favorite saying of the Rabbis of Yavneh was,*
> *"I am a creature of God and my neighbor is also a creature of God. I work in the city and he works in the country. I rise early for my work and he rises early for his work. Just as he cannot excel in my work, I cannot excel in his work. Will you say that I do great things and he does small things? We have learned that it does not matter whether a person does much or little, as long as he directs his heart to heaven."*
> (Berakhot 17a)

There are many ways to destroy a person.[28] When a disabled person cannot be given an honor due to insensitive architecture or leadership we relegate them to secondary status.

We are not being asked to bankrupt the community to provide access – we are being asked to provide access; any step forward is a step we have not yet taken.

There is a difference between not having the money to put in ramps and lower water fountains and refusing to prioritize the changes.

---

[27] The raised platform from which the service is led.
[28] *Lashon Harah*, disrespect and denying them access to the community are all ways in which a person can be destroyed.

Home Work:

1. Investigate the possibility of starting a special "*Minyan Meyuchad*....... (special service in which people with developmental disabilities are active participants) once a month. A 45-minute service, once a month, will bring them into the congregation and go a long way to making them feel like part of the community.
2. Call the non-Jewish service agencies (group homes, etc.) in your area and ask whether there are any Jewish residents who would like to have some contact during the Jewish Holy Days.
3. Visit the local group home or invite the residents to share a meal with you. You will be surprised at how wonderful a time you will have, and how precious an experience it will be for them.
4. Does your congregation/school have a wheelchair, TTY (phone for the deaf), large print prayer books, Braille prayer books or magnifying glasses for prayer books?

Story:

A story of Rabbi Shimon ben Eleazer. He was once coming from Migdal Eder from his master's house, making his way leisurely along the seashore on his donkey, when he saw a man who was exceedingly ugly.

"Wretch!" Rabbi Shimon called to him, "You are very ugly. Are all your townspeople as ugly as you?"

"What can I do?" the man answered.

"Go to the craftsman who made me and say to him how ugly is this vessel you have made!"

No sooner did Rabbi Shimon perceive that he had acted amiss than he got down from the donkey and prostrated himself before the man.

"I beg of you" he said, "Forgive me."

Said the man, "I shall not forgive you until you have gone to the craftsman who made me and say, 'How ugly is this vessel which you have made.'"

Rabbi Shimon ran after him for three miles. The townspeople came forth to meet Rabbi Shimon and hailed him, "Welcome Rabbi."

Said the man to them, "Whom are you calling Rabbi?"

"He that is coming along behind you," said the townspeople.

"If that's a rabbi," he said to them, "May there be no more like him in Israel!"

"Heaven forbid!" they exclaimed. "What did he do to you?"

"Thus and so he did to me."

Said they, "Nevertheless forgive him."

The man replied "For your sake I will forgive him, provided he does not repeat the offense."

(Ta'anit 20)

Community Voices
Integration Is a Two-Way Street
by Nina B. Mogilnik[29]

Integration is a word that rolls easily off the tongue, but when it hits the real world, it often collides with preconceptions, misunderstandings, stubbornness, misguided good intentions, and a whole host of other obstacles.

As the parent of two "typical" children and one autistic child, I pretend no great expertise in the realm of integration. If I am an expert about anything, it is limited to my intimate, hard-won, inside-out knowledge of one particular autistic individual: my son Noah.

Ages and Stages

I vividly recall the many Saturday mornings when my husband and I took Noah to the Tot Shabbat services at our synagogue. Noah would squirm, be inattentive, wander off to play with toys, or just leave the room.

In time, the disconnect between him and the other children grew. Noah couldn't tolerate a more structured and age-appropriate service, so he sat with babies and toddlers in their service until he was about ten years old.

Integration is a funny thing when your child is two or more heads taller and many years older than all the other kids in the room. We had to retrofit Noah into what was available to the general population, or not include him at all.

---

[29] Nina Mogilnik has spent her entire professional life in the nonprofit sector. Her longest tenure was with the Altman Foundation, where she served as Senior Program Officer, and focused on education, social welfare, and the arts. Nina left Altman at the end of 2007 to dedicate more of her time to her children Samuel, Noah and Ariel, and to her husband Len. She is presently a consultant to two family foundations which are focused on the needs of disadvantaged children. Whatever else Nina accomplishes in life, her pride in and affection for her children and her husband will trump all.

Square Peg, Round Hole

Retrofitting could in fact be the tag line for much of our experience of parenting Noah. The world is not really set up to accommodate people with extraordinary needs. Compromise and some form of disappointment seem to be the rule of thumb.

All for One and One for All

If we think about (Jewish) life as a series of concentric circles, at the center of everything is the family, and that is what Noah needed to be integrated into first. It should have been an automatic, seamless task; it was instead one fraught with emotional minefields. We didn't really catch on to Noah's autism, though we wondered about some of his odd behaviors. It was when Noah entered preschool that others sounded the alarm.

Then a process of sputtering acceptance, denial and grieving began in earnest. It was a matter of trying to come to terms with the unexpected, of wrapping our heads around a diagnosis and figuring out how to manage the child who had it, in the context of our family.

That process continues until today, and has been both complicated and enriched by Noah's having two siblings and an extended family. Without charting each gyration in these rela-tionships, suffice it to say that there have been numerous highs and lows. Some of the lows, interestingly, have been around our Jewish life, as have some of the highs.

At home, we have fairly regular Friday night dinners, including the reciting of Kiddush and the lighting of Shabbat candles. Somewhere along the way, Noah learned some of the prayers, so that he led us or joined his sister Ariel in the blessing over the wine and challah. The loveliest tradition *he brought to us* was around the blessing of the children.

Len and I would each bless our children on Shabbat. At some point, Noah decided that he would bless *us*. He blessed us incorrectly, with my receiving the blessing for boys, and Len receiving the blessing for girls. We were meant to point out the mistake and be in on the joke.

Years later, we still do, and we still are.

Beyond the Shabbat Table

This Chanukah, Noah surprised us by reciting the blessings over the candles, which we didn't know he knew. Noah has been building what I would call *Jewish Muscle Memory*. Exposure to and repetition of certain practices at home has become part of the fabric of Noah's being.

Unfortunately, what happens at home cannot easily be mimicked in the outside world. The conditions of home, which include not only fewer people and maximum flexibility, but also unconditional love and acceptance, are rarely if ever found in the outside world.

In the synagogue context, there are big and little barriers, even minute slights. Some years back, an usher chided me because Noah wasn't wearing a *Kippah*. I smiled through slightly clenched teeth and pointed out that my son was not comfortable wearing a *Kippah*. What I wanted to do was scream: "DO YOU REALLY THINK GOD CARES IF THIS CHILD HAS HIS HEAD COVERED? DON'T YOU THINK IT MATTERS MORE THAT HE'S HERE?!?"

Noah quite comfortably wears a kippah now, both at home and in synagogue. Perhaps if we didn't have Shabbat dinners at home, Noah wouldn't wear a kippah. Seeing his older brother Sam and his father each put one on provided incentive, I am sure, for Noah to do the same.

Upping the Educational Ante

Knowing that we lacked the knowledge and wherewithal to provide Noah with a strong Jewish education, we decided to enroll him in the tutorial program of our synagogue's religious school, where Noah was paired with a lovely woman who worked one-on-one with him.

Year one appeared to be a smashing success. Year two was the year of diminishing returns. I found myself sitting outside the classroom each week, listening for that moment when Noah's non-compliance would reach a point where I had to intervene. I realized that as long as Noah had been easygoing and compliant, his teacher could work with him. But she had no skill in managing his behavior. She knew content, but she didn't know my child. End of Hebrew school experiment.

Higher Level Misunderstandings

Sometimes, the scale of misunderstanding is just funny. My "guffaw moment" came when we began the journey toward Noah's becoming a bar mitzvah. The head of our religious school called to tell me that Noah would need to follow the school's curriculum, and that included learning about God. I practically fell off my chair.

"With all due respect," I informed the rabbi, "do you realize that a core deficit in autism is the inability to understand abstractions? And what is more abstract than God?"

A Triumph Among Tribulations

I decided—against my husband's better judgment—that Noah should become a *Bar Mitzvah*. I didn't think about his IQ, his attitude toward non-preferred activities, what could happen if he found himself facing a room full of people, etc. I was given the names of various tutors.

Some weeks later, I found myself in the small chapel just outside our synagogue's main sanctuary. Noah liked to read the Hebrew letters on the memorial plaques that line the walls. We quietly entered, and I watched the tutor with his student.

I saw a patient, gentle man encouraging a struggling student. When they were finished, I approached him. I introduced myself, and asked if he would be interested in working with my son.

Mr. Kerman and Noah sat in the small chapel once a week for months. He re-taught Noah to read Hebrew and then he taught him to chant his *Torah* portion. It is impossible to describe the joy and gratitude I felt as I watched Mr. Kerman sit with his arm around Noah each week, reading with him. Even when Noah was not at his best and didn't want to work, Mr. Kerman never lost his composure.

On May 24, 2009, my autistic son ascended the two steps to the *Bimah* in the little chapel, now filled with family and friends. I heard him say quietly to himself, "I can do it." And when he finished chanting the two *Aliyot* for which Mr. Kerman had prepared him, he said aloud, "I did it." Indeed he did.

Lessons Learned and Not Learned

We decided that Noah should have the same chance at a rite of passage ceremony as anyone else, and *we* identified the person to help us achieve that goal. Our synagogue didn't thwart us, but if Mr. Kerman hadn't been there, I don't think Noah would have reached that day. I suppose we were just lucky.

Noah will be part of the wider world—Jewish or otherwise—to the extent to which we make that a priority, include him in the activities and life of our family, and refuse to accept that he cannot conquer at least some of his limitations. The Jewish community will or will not be part of that, depending on the kind of fit we find between our needs and aspirations for Noah and what the community has to offer.

What Next Then?

The one essential ingredient, above all others, is the imperative *to see the child in front of you for who he is.* That is true for family members, who sometimes see the child they want, rather than the child they have, and it is also true for practitioners of all sorts, who are too often unwilling to admit what they don't know and what they don't understand. Turning away should never be an option. Even if none of us has the answers, we should all feel obligated to ask the right questions.

Community Voices
A Successful Community Beats With One Heart
by Beth Horowitz Giladi[30]

A synagogue is so much more than a physical structure in a community. It is where we as Jews gather to learn, share, grow, grieve, celebrate, care, and share.

After many years in Jewish education and communal work, I have come to an unwavering truth that the more our eyes are opened to something, the more we see real-life examples of that very thing! This is so true with the issue of inclusion of special needs individuals in synagogue life. Synagogues serve a broad constituency and have put forth effort and energy to become the spiritual, communal, and educational center of the members' Jewish world. Historically, though, Jewish children with special needs (and by extension, their families) have not had equal access to these varied and rich offerings.

In recent years, there has been an increase in special needs programming on a community-wide basis which has served to expand offerings to this population. While this enhances their Jewish experiences, it separates these children and families from the rich vibrancy of synagogue life.

There is no argument that outreach efforts to special populations must increase, but without a catalyst to this change process, it is slow going. Hence, this is a guide for opening the conversation with your synagogue so that leaders and members alike will begin to see what has been missing and how it can be addressed. This will not be an exhaustive list of programs and projects for two reasons: one is that

---

[30] Beth Horowitz Giladi, MSW, LCSW, has been involved in Jewish special education programming for more than 25 years. She has created inclusion programs for day and residential camps, religious schools, synagogues, and communities. The founding director of the Metrowest NJ Jewish Education Association's Department of Special Education, she has worked with professional groups and parents to facilitate creative collaborations. Currently, Beth is a Social Worker in a NJ public school district and is the Founding Director of P.E.A.C.E. at Home (Parent Education and Coaching for Excellence).

those resources already exist in the Jewish community and can be easily accessed, and two, I believe it isn't so much the "how" to make an inclusive community that must be shared. It is much more the "why" we should and "what" it will offer to each of us. Once you're a believer, the path becomes evident.

First Steps:

Join (or approach) your synagogue with the intention of actualizing a connection for yourself or your children with special needs. It is not solely the responsibility of special needs families to make their synagogue inclusive, so reach out your hand to the professional staff and membership to make that journey together. Work with others to sensitize the synagogue family to issues of inclusion.

Learn about the current synagogue structure of committees and how programs develop so that your ideas are wedded to the congregation's goals and mission. Organic growth based on the established goals is the most likely kind of change to be sustained. "Each one teach one" can be a model for how to bring people on the mission. Lead the charge, but feel confident bringing up the stragglers. Flexibility in thought and planning will allow for change in the fabric of synagogue life, slowly, gradually, and with assurance that intent (and not perfection) is the goal.

Begin by assessing: what does the synagogue need to learn? To know? To experience? Form a committee of like-minded individuals so you are not carrying the burden by yourself. By collaborating with other families of children or adults with special needs, the loneliness and feeling self-conscious about reaching for change will be transformed to a sense of belonging and a feeling of purpose.

Communicate:

Many grassroots efforts at change are initiated and propelled forward by family members. Reach out to the membership for experienced educators, mental health professionals, collaborators, and caring families. The community's wealth is in its human resources. Once you have a committee for increasing inclusion, begin to plant seeds of awareness. A monthly column in the synagogue bulletin can be a powerful tool. Sometimes the column should include educational articles to increase understanding of various disabilities, and sometimes personal narratives from families about their synagogue experience with their special needs family member. The personal narrative can be a powerful message. Offer a series of "town meetings" in homes or the synagogue as an opportunity for people to hear one another's stories – of struggle, isolation, pride, and belonging.

Introduce a common vocabulary about special needs and the type of community and add it to all synagogue literature.

Interact And Integrate:

For special needs families, *Shabbat* is often a frustrating and disappointing time in the synagogue. Spiritual nourishment is hard to experience when you are worried about the disruption caused by a family member and the subsequent rejection by the congregants present. We simply must embrace Jews in our midst even when their behavior challenges our own definition of acceptable acts.

Be the change agent who will sit with a family whose son or daughter has special needs and help them see that they are unconditionally accepted and welcome. Sometimes, an older or more experienced *Shabbat* "regular" can act as a *Shabbat* Buddy. Perhaps a parent is not available or not comfortable, so a *Shabbat* Buddy is the one who will sit with the child and facilitate his participation. Obviously they stay only as long as it is a positive experience for the child. Work with clergy to incorporate family meal-sharing. Host a family in your home for *Shabbat* dinner. Your child will be most comfortable in his environment and you can take the opportunity to de-mystify your child's behaviors and model helpful interventions.

While integration in services is important, special prayer services tailored to the developmental needs of the participants, to which all congregants are invited, addresses the needs of some. Without regard for age, all family members are included. Rarely does attendance at these services leave the congregant the same as before they went: we are all transformed by the experience of shared joy.

Find ways for your family member with special needs to make a contribution to the synagogue's efforts: join a community service project that offers an opportunity to participate. This boost to self esteem also highlights the "can do," not the "can't" for the special needs individual and everyone else present.

Become Part of the Community:

Life cycle events are woven into the fabric of synagogue life: a baby naming, *Bnai Mitzvah*, marriage ceremonies, and rituals and observances surrounding death. Participating in these rites of passage is not a "charitable act" the synagogue performs. It is a birthright of all community members and an opportunity for sharing. We all learn something when a special needs child achieves something or performs a ritual function after a great deal of practice. Every congregant learns something when the parent of a special needs child raises an issue about removing a barrier to participation so that all children are included.

Central to Jewish teachings is a mandate to treat every person with dignity and respect.

> *Teach every person according to his way.*
> *(Proverbs 22:6)*

As a parent, you will likely have to play the role of educator to articulate your child's needs. What your child will need, how it should be provided, when, where, and with who are all questions that are pivotal to a child's successful integration in the religious school. Ignorance should not be equated with lack of interest.

Operate from the premise that synagogues are communities and communities are inclusive. Everyone belongs, but we may need to show the way to actualize that belief. Acknowledge approximate steps on the path to inclusion so that you aren't focusing solely on the outcome.

Educate:

Jewish education is rooted in this text:

> *All your children shall be students of The Lord*
> *(Isaiah 54:13)*

The efforts to include children with special needs are vital. Begin early and make a realistic appraisal of the possible interface points: where, and in what ways your child can join what is already in place in the synagogue: early childhood programming, *Shabbat* events, religious school classes in part or full, and youth groups. Finding appropriate supports (teen aide, shadow, co-teaching situation) may make the difference between success and failure. Use what the secular school has already learned about your child to create a mirror support program in religious school. Foster open communication and support, allowing the religious school educator to speak with the personnel from the secular school to identify educational and behavioral interventions that may facilitate success. Identifying areas and skills that your child will only be able to master with individualized or specialized instruction (Hebrew language, for example) is part of this process. Be sure to see what resources are in your midst: older congregants, former educators, and empty-nesters can be wonderful assistants or 1:1 aides in school activities. Finally, the new technology: the digital recordings and audio CDs, for example, can be used to facilitate learning. There are numerous publications and manuals for ways to make the religious school program inclusive. We do not need to re-invent the wheel. *Al Pi Darco: According to Their Ways* by the URJ, written in 2000, is just one example of such a resource which is filled with wonderful information.

Engage the school administrator to look ahead to events and explore how your child might participate. If the child's school shadow were to stand on the *Bima* with him/her during a play or an assembly, would that suffice? Does one of the parents need to ascend along with their child in order to facilitate his involvement? Is it better for the child to sit in a row of the congregation rather than in the public eye on the *Bima*? Seeking solutions is a contact sport, so *put everyone on the team!*

Be Positive:

Sharing an experience with a special needs individual, witnessing someone master something through intense effort or feeling joy together in a celebration leaves an indelible mark in the minds and hearts of synagogue members. It is a win-win outcome which leaves everyone richer, having shared a spiritual encounter. Encourage your synagogue members to join in the journey of inclusion. Encourage them to seek ways to connect to each other so that none of us is found "knee deep in the river and dying of thirst" with undiscovered opportunities which pass our way without our noticing. Join with them in opening ears, eyes, and hearts to the possibilities for inclusion. Create teachable moments that bring everyone to a deeper understanding and inter-connectedness and then reflect on what has transpired.

> *"For truly to see your face is like seeing the face of God"*   *(Genesis 33:10)*

You will be part of a community transformed.

Section Three: Tzedakah: Introduction

American Jews have an idealized conception of the Land of Israel. Too many of us travel to Israel expecting to witness Israelis dancing *Horas* in the streets extolling the virtues of Zionism and studying Torah. We expect Israelis to act on the highest of moral levels because they embody the ideals we teach. An American tourist arriving in Israel full with expectations can be easily disillusioned. Israel is a place where wondrous things happen and miracles occur daily but it is populated by human beings who do human things.[31]

In one trip to Israel I was praying at the *Kotel* (the Wailing Wall in Jerusalem) when a man approached and asked me to help make the tenth for *Minyan*. It is not a request that can be refused so I walked over to this group to make the *Minyan*. I was given an honor to bless the *Torah* and afterwards the *Gabbai* (one of the men running the *Minyan*) asked for ten dollars. He explained that I owed him the money for the honor he had given me. When I refused he told me it was for *Tzedakah* and that I was a bad Jew for not giving when asked. I knew better and walked away.

But, I was intrigued. I went a distance away and watched. It was a nice day and there were plenty of tourists in the plaza. There were two *Gabbais* at this one table; one brought people over while the other did the blessings and collected the money. I watched for over an hour and asked several people who had donated how much they had given. In that one hour fifteen people gave at least ten dollars each, one other person had refused.

When I asked one of the donors if he realized that he was not required to give money for a blessing, he replied that it felt good to give money to *Tzedakah* at the *Kotel*.

But was he giving *Tzedakah*? No donor knew where the money was going. They didn't know what it would be used for. Could they have refused? They didn't think so.

---

[31] I relate the following story hoping it will successfully illustrate the need for the following section of the Laws of *Tzedakah* without disillusionment.

We are known as "The People of the Book." We have laws for everything, *Tzedakah* too. Most people don't know there are laws governing the giving and use of *Tzedakah*. They are important because knowledge of the law would help the giver be more discerning and determine when giving is at their discretion and when it is not. It would also help avoid situations where an unknown person can prey upon the naïve tourist and take money for undetermined purposes.

Chapter 16: *Tzedakah* - The Dynamics of Giving

It was taught in the name of Rabbi Yehoshua: The poor person standing at the door does more for the householder than the householder does for the poor person. (Vayikra Rabbah 34:8)

Sacrifice is usually something people get angry over, if when you sacrifice for someone you become obsessed with what you have lost. But sacrifice is a part of life. It's supposed to be. It's not something to regret, it's something to aspire to.
(Rachel Naomi Remen)

Good People: Dr. Eliezer Jaffe

Dr. *Eliezer* Jaffe is one of the best *Tzedakah* teachers. Born in America, he moved to Israel more than thirty years ago. A social worker, he became a professor of social work at Hebrew University in Jerusalem and has taught students to see Israeli society with its virtues and vices. He specializes in modeling how people working together can make a difference in Israeli life.

He knows and understands what we call "grassroots *Tzedakah*" and has organized many groups. His most famous one is the Israel Free Loan Association, which has lent out millions of dollars to people in need…with no interest and no extra costs when the borrower repays the loan. "Free Loan" means exactly that: they lend out money at no cost.

Dr. Jaffe has worked to change government policy so that the lives of immigrants, large families, people with disabilities and those who want to adopt children can have better lives.

He is someone we can learn from, someone who can show us the way to use our talent and money wisely for *Tikun Olam*.

*   *   *

Several yeas ago I went to visit one of my daughters in Israel. She was attending a summer program and had one Shabbat free in Jerusalem. Friday afternoon several families took their daughters to *Ben*

Yehuda Street[32] to prepare for Shabbat.

As a group we were beset by beggars asking for money. Some would give a few "*shek*"[33] or like me, they would turn away. One young American male, dressed in Chasidic garb, persisted. I finally asked him, "why are you asking for money?" He answered, "I have nothing to eat for *Shabbat*."

Immediately that changed the entire dynamic.[34] I told him I would not give him money but would buy him his three meals for *Shabbat*. He left, to return ten minutes later with his roommate. To the consternation of the other families and the utter surprise of these two boys, I took them to the nearest "take out place" and bought them three meals for *Shabbat*.

When they were about to leave, laden with their food (and beer), one asked me why I spent so much money on them. I told him that since he had asked for food I was not allowed to refuse. He had never heard of that law, and asked me to educate him.

I replied, "I am a Conservative Rabbi, I know that you will not accept Jewish law from me."

He answered, "But you know about the laws of *Tzedakah*."

I smiled and said, "Now I know the *Mashiach* (Messiah) is near," a sentiment to which he heartily agreed.

Our tradition downplays the importance of intention in favor of action. You are, and you are judged by what you do, not what you intend to do. There are exceptions to this rule, one of them is *Tzedakah*. At first glance *Tzedakah* seems simple: someone gives money to someone else. However *Tzedakah* is not only what you give, but how you give it as well.

---

[32] Friday afternoon on *Ben Yehuda* Street is an experience not to be missed. In the summer you might meet friends from your hometown, your rabbi or see different groups of *Hasidim*. Everyone, though, is busy preparing for *Shabbat*.

[33] One "*Shek*," short for "*Shekel*" was worth about twenty five cents at the time.

[34] As you will read later on, according to Jewish law, when a person specifically asks for food, their needs must be met.

> *A rabbi saw a man give a zuz to a beggar publicly. He said to him, "better you had given him nothing than give him something and put him to shame."* (Chagigah 5a)

The way *Tzedakah* is offered is as important as the offer itself. If the money is offered in a way that humiliates the recipient, then it is not *Tzedakah*. What good is the money if there is no self-respect to go with it? People in need have feelings and dignity as well.

Yet, are we not all approached by panhandlers in public? Does this text imply that any money given in public is wrong? We distinguish between what is given and how it is given. If you are approached in public it is fitting to give in public. However, if you could give in private or if the person has standing in the community, you must give in such a way that the recipient does not feel humiliated.

The Politics of Giving:

One of the more troubling aspects of *Tzedakah* is its tendency to be coercive. I often hear people who are turned off by different community institution's policy of publicizing the names of donors to "encourage" others to give. The practice goes back to the middle ages and before. I myself have been disenchanted by these tactics from time to time.

I was once asked to be on the board of a local charitable organization. At the first meeting, we were each handed a binder with informational material. Within the material was one page; the left column had the name of each board member. The next three columns listed in order; address and phone number, last year's contribution and this year's recommended contribution.

It was my last board meeting.

> *Members of a community may force each other to build a synagogue and to buy a Torah, the Prophets and the Writings.*
> (Shulchan Aruch, Orach Chaim 150:1)

Despite this experience, I would like to reframe this issue in the following way: Is it that the members of our community have the **right** to force others to contribute or is it that the members of our community have the **obligation** to force others to contribute to *Tzedakah*?

There is a difference between "right" and "obligation." To me this issue highlights the conflict of values of Jews living in the United States. The United States is a country that values individual freedom. In contrast, Jewish law emphasizes the priority of community.

Our community uses coercion in many forms:

1. Open any bulletin or newsletter from a congregation. How are the donations publicized. How many are from "anonymous?"
2. Take a walk around your congregation/school. How many plaques do you see?
3. Make a donation to any charitable organization. Wait three months. How many brochures and solicitations are you getting by mail?
4. How many times is the memory of the Holocaust invoked to motivate giving?
5. How many times are the donors identified during a fund raising event.

In my first congregation, in Greenbelt, Maryland, we prided ourselves on never announcing a donor during the High Holy Day appeal. There was never one piece of paper with the names of donors identified. We were lucky to raise $10,000 from 200 families. One year, the leadership gave the donors the "option" of being identified. We raised $20,000. It was however, the only year of this custom. Too many people felt "coerced" by having to keep up with their neighbors. The congregation suffered accordingly.

For me, the "bottom line" of this *Mitzvah* is that if the money will directly affect people in need – and not go to umbrella organizations with administrative costs and building funds, any form of coercion is allowed. Any other organization must weigh its tactics with the percentage of monies it actually spends on the programs it supports.

> *Rabbi Eleazar said, "Greater is he who persuades others to give than him who gives..." He who gives charity in secret is as great as Moses.*
> *(Bava Batra, 8 - 9)*

Tzedakah can be a big business. It takes a lot of money to help people in big ways. There are many organizations that employ professional fundraisers to raise large sums of money for their projects. But, there is a difference between *Tzedakah* and fundraising. *Tzedakah* is when you take a resource and transfer it to someone else for that person's benefit. It is a direct transaction. Fundraising is the raising of money for a *Tzedakah* cause. There is a difference.

If you give $1,000 to a *Tzedakah* cause, you may have only given $500 to *Tzedakah*. There is "overhead." "Overhead" is the amount of money taken from the funds raised that is used to pay the bills. If you add the rent, salaries, utilities and all other costs, $1,000 can easily become $500 or much, much less. I left the board of that charitable organization I mentioned above not solely because of its coercive method – but because I looked around and saw too many staff members, expensive binders and high overhead expenses.

Before you give *Tzedakah*, you should ask questions. As with any other business, the motto is "buyer beware!"

1. How do they use their funds?
2. How did you find out about them?
3. What are the funds used for?
4. How do you know they are honest?
5. Who recommends them?
6. Are they ultimately concerned with dignity and compassion
7. Do they operate on a cash basis?

There are websites[35] dedicated to keeping *Tzedakah* organizations honest. They are easily accessible and user friendly.

---

[35] Go to http://www.just-tzedakah.org or www.charitynavigator.org

Arrogance and *Tzedakah*:

Tzedakah is more than a handout. It is more than just writing and mailing a check. It is an action that is designed to build a caring community. If done right, it can change the way you look at the world and your responsibilities to it – and that can change the world. That is why the *"ways"* of giving *Tzedakah* are as important as the giving itself.

Tzedakah is not complicated, people are. We must be sensitive to the people we are helping or we defeat the needs we attempt to fulfill. When a teacher offers a poor child lunch money in front of the class she does more harm than good. What good is delivering food that has to be cooked to a poor family without a kitchen? How effective is having a small sign in a synagogue lobby that says "Large Print Siddurim at the bottom of the shelf?"

But we resist. For whatever reason there are too many people who find too many reasons not to care. There is an arrogance in that attitude. What I mean is when you are so full of yourself there is no room in your world for anyone else.

> *Adam was created (last) on the eve of the Shabbat. Why? So that if a person becomes too proud, one can say to him, "The gnat was created before you."*
> *(Sanhedrin 38a)*

While there is an arrogance in those who solicit funds and there is also an arrogance in those who refuse to give. There is also an arrogance in those who refuse to accept the help when it is needed.

> *Whoever cannot survive without taking Tzedakah such as an old, sick or greatly suffering individual, but who stubbornly refuses to accept aid, is guilty of murdering himself.*
> *(Shulchan Aruch, Yoreh Deah 255:2)*

There are certain experiences I will never forget. One such

experience was when the person in charge of our synagogue kitchen came to me with a complaint; someone was stealing food. She had caught him in the act. He had come in on a Friday afternoon and taken from the Shabbat dinner being prepared that evening. I knew the family in question and I knew their circumstance. They were house-poor.[36] I made it my business to see him that week and explained to him that I would get all the food he needed when he needed it. However, he couldn't take from the synagogue kitchen because he would be caught – and I didn't want him to be caught. He angrily denied the incident and informed me that there was enough of everything in his house.

I still feel guilty that I couldn't do more to help his children.

> *In Vilna a wealthy man lost all he had. He was greatly ashamed of being poor. He informed no one of his situation and eventually died of starvation. Rabbi Salanter consoled the ashamed townspeople. "That man did not die of starvation, but of excessive pride. Had he been willing to ask others to help and admit his situation, he would not have died of hunger."*

Another experience was when I became involved with the Jewish Family Service (JFS) of New Orleans and saw how much sensitivity is required at times for *Tzedakah*. The year after Hurricane Katrina, our congregation volunteered to provide funds for *Maot Chittin*. The professionals at the JFS asked us if we could send people to deliver the food. We collected $10,000 from the congregation and 23 members of our congregation paid their own way to NOLA (New Orleans, Louisiana). JFS bought the food from local kosher vendors. We packaged it and delivered it.

That evening, after we had finished, I asked the JFS professional why she wanted us to deliver it. Her answer taught me how

---

[36] A condition that arises from buying a house that is too expensive for your budget. All the money goes for the mortgage, taxes and utilities. As a result there is nothing left for food and clothing.

wonderfully sensitive she was, how caring NOLA's Jewish organizations were and a lot about *Tzedakah*. She said that many of the people receiving food this year had delivered it to others in past years. Had she and her volunteers delivered it this year, the embarrassment of receiving the food from people they knew well would have been too much to handle. So, strangers were asked to perform the task. That is *Tzedakah* in action.

Our tradition places great emphasis upon our willingness to give to those in need and our ability to accept the support of others when we are in need. A community cannot exist unless there is a natural give and take in the dynamic of the community; sometimes you give and sometimes you take.

And we must be mature. Just because we have been humiliated in the past does not give us permission to allow the dynamic to continue.

> *No one should say, "Just as I have been humiliated so too let others be humiliated."*
> (Bereshit Rabbah 24)

I also believe that denial of a problem is a form of arrogance. Is ignoring a glaring need in our community a subtle way of humiliating others? For example, does refusal to provide wheelchair access constitute humiliation of those who now cannot participate fully in the service?

Home Work:

1. Make it a family activity to peruse the newspaper to identify all the articles and advertisements that illustrate some sort of *Tzedakah* work.

2. Discuss this story from Eli Wiesel:

   Traveling along the Nile we saw many beggar children asking for money. I saw one lady throwing pennies to them. They crowded near her, jostling for position, beating each other in a mad scramble for money. I begged her, "Please do not throw money to them."

She replied, "but I love to give charity."

3. As a family, write up a list of the *Ten Commandments of Tzedakah*. Observe them.

Story:

    Once, on a bitter cold night, Rabbi Yosef was teaching his students, he heard a knock on his door. It was Baruch; a very poor student with a wife and new child at home. He looked desperate.

    "Rabbi, I haven't earned much these last weeks. We don't have enough money to heat our home. It is so cold and I am afraid that my wife and baby will suffer. What can I do?"

    Rabbi Yosef gave him what he had. He sent him to buy some coal and told him he would be out to see him soon. After Baruch left, his students asked him what he intended to do.

    "I am going to see Reb Nissin," was the reply.

    Reb Nissin was the wealthiest man in town – but also the most miserly. No one had ever been able to get him to give to anyone or anything.

    Rabbi Yosef went up to his door, with his students watching from afar. He knocked on Reb Nissin's door. The servant answered the door. When he saw it was Reb Nissin he invited him in but Rabbi Yosef declined. He would wait outside. After a few minutes Reb Nissin appeared.

    "Rabbi Yosef, what are you waiting outside for? Come in and warm yourself. Then we can talk."

    "No thank you. I don't want to be a bother. I just have a simple question to ask."

    Reb Nissin, shivering in the cold, again pleaded with him. "There is no need to be so uncomfortable."

    Again Rabbi Yosef declined. "I don't want to be a bother." He continued. "There is a poor student who lives not far from here who needs money to heat his home. Do you think you could help him out?"

    Reb Nissin dug deeply into his pockets and came up with a very generous sum. He told Rabbi Yosef, "Please take this to him. Tell him to come around tomorrow if he needs some work. I will see what I can do."

    His students were amazed.

    "Rabbi Yosef," they cried, "How did you do it? How did you get Reb

Nissin to contribute?"

Reb Yosef answered, "Reb Nissin lives in a warm house. He does not know hunger. He does not know pain. I knew if I could only get him to feel the cold he would learn how to give."

Chapter 17: *Tzedakah* The First Step

Tzedakah is equal in importance to all the other commandments combined. (Baba Batra 9a)

The tragedy in life doesn't lie in not reaching your goal. The tragedy lies in having no goal to reach.
(Benjamin Mays)

Each *Bar/Bat Mitzvah* at our congregation receives a set of candlesticks from Sisterhood, a kiddush cup from Men's Club, one year's membership in our youth group, a *Tzedakah* box[37] from the congregation and a book by Danny Siegel entitled *Heroes and Miracle Workers* from me. The gifts are symbolic of the foundational values of our tradition and immediately useable. While this ritual is carried out at many *Bnai Mitzvah* in other congregations each week, few other congregations present a *Tzedakah* box. We decided to give the box because over the years we have found that many people just don't know how to take the first step and make *Tzedakah* a priority in their lives.

It's not a lack of knowledge. We all know there are people in need. Every educational institution teaches it, it is plastered over the media and clergy speak about it from the *bimah* all the time. In these last decades we have seen the technology of communication bring the world into our palms. The world is smaller and so, it seems, are we. We have become insignificant members of a global community and have learned that one person doesn't count for very much. There is a hedonism that has perpetuated our society. Yet one person can make a difference.

The internet gives us access to people all over the world helping us to learn about so many other places. Technology has made it so simple to help others. Now when a family has an extra pair of crutches we can contact an organization called *Yad Sarah* in Israel to see if they need another pair. We send a notice to our membership to see if they know of anyone traveling to Israel. Within just one single day we have arranged for the donation, transportation and delivery.

---

[37] I recognize that to some a Tzedakah box would be considered "*muktzah*," something that should not be touched on Shabbat – it is not.

Using email we can contact hundreds of people to tell them we are collecting school supplies for the Ethiopian community in Israel. We can collect the supplies and arrange for the participants in our congregational trip to Israel to carry one extra duffel filled with school supplies. We can arrange for the duffels to be picked up from our hotel in Israel – and $4,000 worth of crayons, markers, paper, glue, art supplies and much more have been delivered.

The list is endless. So, we give the *Tzedakah* box to each *Bnai Mitzvah* in our congregation because the first step in giving *Tzedakah* is just that, to give.

> *When Rabbi Yehoshua ben Levi went to Rome he saw marble pillars covered with sheets so they wouldn't crack from the heat, nor freeze from the cold. He also saw a poor person with only a reed mat under him and another one on his back.*
> *(Pesikta D'Rav Kahana 9:1)*

In its day, Rome was the most powerful and most civilized nation on earth. Its architecture was famous world over. The Romans cared for their buildings more than they cared for their people. Marble pillars are expensive. People weren't.

How can we say our society is different?

Story:

Rabbi Ya'akov Yitzchak was one day walking on the road and came across a peasant whose cart full of straw had overturned.

"Greetings, brother," the peasant cried. "Come help me right my cart."

The Rabbi looked at the cart with its thick solid wooden walls and its heavy wooden wheels. He shook his head.

"I'd like to help you but I can't. I'm not strong enough." He turned to go, but the peasant shouted.

"Yes you can, but you don't want to."

Rabbi Ya'akov Yitzchak was stunned by these harsh words and determined to prove the peasant wrong. He took off his coat and together with the peasant went into the nearby woods to cut saplings for levers. They hitched the horse to the side of the cart, put the poles beneath the side and began to lift. At a word from the peasant, the horse began to pull and then heave. Nothing happened at first. Then little by little, their combined efforts began to tell. Slowly the wagon began to turn, and then in a little while they had it on its wheels. In silence the two men collected the spilled straw and loaded it back on the wagon. They set off in the same direction and as they went, the Rabbi asked,

"Brother, how did you know that I could help you?"

The peasant laughed. "I didn't know any more than you knew that your efforts would fail."

"How did you know that I didn't want to help you?"

"That's easy. I knew you didn't want to because you didn't try."

(As told by Martin Buber.)

A letter to you, the reader:

Dear Reader:

As you know, one of the goals of this book is to teach about the concept of Tzedakah. As a project we would like you to begin collecting all the loose change that accumulate throughout the house. At the end of each month we would like you donate what you have found to a worthy cause.

Could you set up a container somewhere in the house to collect the change?

Thank you for your cooperation.

Steven Bayar, Rabbi

Community Voices
Involving Your Children in Tzedakah Decisions
by Diane Lipszyc[38]

Start a child on the right road... (Proverbs 22:6)

Like a number of children of Holocaust survivors, I grew up on an egg farm in southern New Jersey. My father would put on a special sports jacket to attend the Jewish Poultry Farmer's Association meetings. The men would solicit each other for the United Jewish Appeal campaign. One of my earliest recollections about *Tzedakah* is my dad telling me that he gave a check for his pledge, but since the chickens had yet to lay their eggs, he asked his solicitor to please wait before turning the check over to UJA. I loved helping my mom make calls to remind fellow *Hadassah* women of an upcoming meeting. While my parents didn't involve my brothers and myself in their tzedakah decisions, they set a wonderful example and showed the importance of *Tzedakah*.

Once my husband and I became parents, we also wanted to teach our children the importance of *Tzedakah*. Naturally, the importance of giving was reinforced by teachings at our synagogue, Jewish Day School, and summer camps. Whether donating food to a local pantry, participating in our synagogue's "*Mitzvah* Day" or helping out at our Federation's Super Sunday, they learned about *Tzedakah* in many forms.

Moreover, when each became a *Bar* or *Bat Mitzvah*, they chose meaningful *Tzedakah* projects to fund. Our eldest child chose to buy and donate *Passover* food to recent immigrants. Our next child, the book lover, bought new books to donate to three local educational and child welfare organizations. She also asked members of our synagogue to donate lightly used books to those organizations. Our youngest child became a *Bat Mitzvah* shortly after the economic crisis in Argentina in the

---

[38] Diane Lipszyc was born in Vineland, NJ to Holocaust survivors from Radom, Poland. During her teen years, she was extremely active in United Synagogue Youth and then went on to become staff at Camp Ramah in New England and study at Hebrew University in Jerusalem . She met her husband at a Federation picnic and together they have raised three wonderful "*mensches.*"

early 2000s. She donated all her *Bat Mitzvah* money to the Jewish community in Argentina through the American Jewish Joint Distribution Committee.

It is our family tradition to give *Tzedakah* at *Hanukkah* time. Our children did not receive many tangible gifts from us, but they did receive funds to allocate to others. Our children understood that with the arrival of *Hanukkah* and its gift-giving custom, they had to make lists of organizations that they would like to contribute to. From an early age, we taught our children not only about the importance of *Tzedakah* as a concept, but also showed them how to research and find organizations that were appropriate to fund. These are examples of sites that they (and others) can use in researching organizations that may merit *Tzedakah* dollars:

http://www.guidestar.org/
http://www.charitynavigator.org/
http://geatnonprofits.org/

Unlike my parents, who simply led by example, my husband and I chose to actively bring our children into important family *Tzedakah* initiatives. For example, when we decided to make a substantial gift to our Synagogue and I had a particular fund in mind, our children persuasively argued that we should direct the funds to the youngest members in the community. As a result of their input, we funded the nursery school at our congregation, which now bears the names of our three children.

Now that our twenty-something children are out on their own, I send them a "*Tzedakah* reminder" email in November to begin thinking where they would like to give. It's our gift to them.

Chapter 18: *Tzedakah* - The Law

*As fish die when they are out of the water, so do people
die without law and order. (Avodah Zarah 4)*

*Our main business is not to see what lies dimly at a
distance, but to do what lies clearly at hand. (Thomas Carlyle)*

There are so many misconceptions about *Tzedakah*: how do we give it, when do we give it, how is it to be used?. Few people know that there are laws governing this *Mitzvah*. Below is a sample of the laws of *Tzedakah* taken from the *Shulchan Aruch*, the most accepted code of Jewish law.[39] My commentary is written in italics.

Chapter #247: The Reward of *Tzedakah* is Great

a. It is a positive *Mitzvah*[40] to give *Tzedakah*.

b. It also involves a negative *Mitzvah* concerning "Averting one's eyes from it"[41] (ignoring the need)…Each person who "averts his eye"…is as though he were an *idolater*.

Idolatry involves putting another god (or value) before the One God. *Refusing to recognize the necessity and obligation of Tzedakah is equated with showing disrespect to God's creations. Literally, your money is more important to you than helping another human being.*

c. It is important to beware, for it is possible for a person to *cause a death*, that the poor person will die if you do not give to him immediately…

How can a person who refuses to give Tzedakah be considered a murderer? When you don't take care of people who are in

---

[39] Written by Joseph Caro in the 16th Century.
[40] A positive *Mitzvah* is a *Mitzvah* that one does: giving Tzedakah, eating matzah, shaking a lulav. A negative *Mitzvah* is a *Mitzvah* that one does not do: do not murder, do not cheat, do not bear false witness.
[41] Averting one's eye is another way of saying, "Do not stand idly by" *(Bal Tashchit)*.

need, they die. They may not die immediately but they will die sooner, than if you helped them.

d. No one is ever too poor to give *Tzedakah*...

e. God takes pity with every person who has pity on the poor.

f. *Tzedakah* will combat the harsh decrees (of God) and during famine will save from death...

g. It is forbidden to *test God* except in this matter...

By far the most interesting part of this text is the phrase "It is forbidden to test God except in this matter." We are specifically forbidden to make deals with God; to say "God, I will perform this Mitzvah if you will _____(fill in the blank)." [42] The only exception in all of Jewish law is when giving Tzedakah. we are allowed to say, "I give Tzedakah on the condition that you, God, will _____ (fill in the blank)."[43]

Chapter 248: Who is Responsible to Give? Who is Fitting to Receive?

a. Everyone is required to give *Tzedakah*. Even one who is poor and is supported by *Tzedakah* is required to give from what he receives...

One would not believe this, but, even poor people are required to give Tzedakah. They too are part of the community and bear a responsibility for those in need. We also begin to see that Tzedakah is

---

[42] The reason given is that sometimes the answer is "no," and people might lose faith if their prayers are not answered to their satisfaction.
[43] Two examples come to mind; the *Mi Sheberach* (prayer said for one who is ill), where we say "May the One who blessed our ancestors....help and heal this person because I am donating *Tzedakah* on their behalf. Also, in the traditional *El Moleh* prayer (for the deceased) we say, "May the All Merciful One grant perfect peace to the soul of our loved one...because I donate *Tzedakah* on their behalf.

more than giving aid to those in need, it is a fundamental building block of our community. As such, it serves a purpose in creating and perpetuating values.

There is also the issue of self-respect. One of the most effective ways to build self esteem in a person is to empower them to help others. Those at the bottom of the economic chain, those who need our help to survive are required to help others – and thereby given the opportunity to acquire self respect from the action. They can see themselves as contributors to the community.

b. One who gives less than what is the acceptable amount, the *Beit Din* (Rabbinic Court) can punish him with blows for being a rebellious person until he gives, and his assets may be taxed in front of him as they take from him what is appropriate to give…

A "rebellious person" is one who refuses to support the community and the Rabbinic Court is given the power to coerce them into cooperating. Remember, at the time this code was written the Jewish community was self-governing internally and could not rely on the external government. There was no welfare, unemployment benefits or Social Security mandated by law. All we had was each other.

c. Orphans are not required to give *Tzedakah* even for ransoming the captives, even if they have sufficient funds…

d. A man who gives more money that he can afford or if he gives too much in order not to be embarrassed…the *Gabbai* is not allowed to take *Tzedakah* from him…

Chapter #251: To Whom Do We Give *Tzedakah*? Who Takes Priority?

a. For one who purposefully violates each and every of the many *Mitzvot* of the *Torah*, and has not repented, there is no responsibility to support him.

b. However, we support the poor of the idolaters with the poor of Israel to keep the peace.

c. One who gives to his father, if he is in need of the support, =is given priority before others. Not only that but he must give him priority before others.

d. Even if he (the one in need) is not his father or he (the donor) his son but just a relative he must take priority over anyone else.

e. The poor of his house take precedence to the poor of his town.

f. The poor of his town take precedence of the poor of another town…

g. Those who dwell in the land of Israel take precedence of the poor who dwell in other countries…

h. One who is hungry takes precedence over one who is naked…

i. A woman takes precedence over a man…

j. A female orphan takes precedence over a male orphan…

k. If there were many poor before him and he does not have the resources to support them all, a *Kohen* takes precedence over a *Levi*, a *Levi* to a *Yisrael*, a *Yisrael* to a *Chalal*…

l. This is the case when they are all equal in wisdom. However a scholar takes precedence…even if the scholar needs clothing and the peasant needs food.

In theory one who consciously rebels against the community and recognizes no responsibility to it receives no support from the community. Although you will note that the law states that they must "violate each and every of the many Mitzvot," suggesting that in practice no one really fits into this category.

What can you do with limited funds? To me, the primary import of this text is that an order was established. The order clearly shows the priority of values in the Jewish community of that time: it is designed to create maximum continuity. Thus, a scholar, because of his knowledge and his ability to use it takes precedence over everyone else. Knowledge and its transmission from generation to generation insures our survival.

Chapter #255: Stay Far Away from Needing *Tzedakah*:

a. A person should try as hard as possible not to need *Tzedakah*...

b. Even a scholar who is honored should work in crafts rather than accept funds.

c. Anyone who needs to take money and cannot live without it should take: i.e. an aged person, or a sick person...

d. If he doesn't take the funds this is like murder and he is responsible for his own life.

Home Work:

1. Take a look at text #251, the order of priority in the case of limited funds. Discuss as a family; do you agree? What would your order be?

Chapter 19: *Tzedakah:* Maimonides' Eight Degrees of *Tzedakah*

While this is arguably the most popular text about *Tzedakah* in our tradition I find it strangely problematic. This in no way is meant to impugn or show disrespect to one of the greatest minds and leaders of the Jewish community: Maimonides. However, I don't think it was meant to be taken as "gospel." Rather, I think it was intended to be an easily understandable reference text.

The text consists of eight sentences given in ascending order of what Maimonides suggests were the degrees of giving *Tzedakah*.[44] Let's look at them in order:

> *There are eight degrees of Tzedakah, one higher than the other. (The lowest is) One who gives ungraciously.*
>
> *The next degree is that of he who gives less than is fitting but gives graciously.*

I would reverse these two. I recognize that to disagree with Maimonides might be considered the height of *Chutzpah*, however my disagreement comes because of personal experience. Some years ago I had two *Tzedakah* appointments. The first appointment was quick, as soon as I started to speak he interrupted me in a gruff voice and said,

"How much do you want?"

I named a figure. He wrote a check and told me to leave. I left feeling humiliated.

What ensued in the next appointment made me feel worse. I met with the potential donor for forty five minutes. We got to know each other. He was warm and listened to what I had to say very carefully. After half an hour he asked me how much I needed. When I told him, he quartered it, citing reasons I knew to be false. I left feeling more

---

[44] They are found in the *Mishneh Torah,* Laws concerning Gifts to the Poor, 7 – 14.

soiled than from the first experience. The first man was gruff, but honest and giving. He was unpleasant but wrote the check. The second experience made me feel as though I was being used.

> *The next degree is that of he who gives only after the poor person asks.*
>
> *The next degree is of he who, with his own hand, bestows a gift before the poor person asks.*
>
> *The next degree is that in which the poor person knows from whom he is taking but the giver knows not to whom he is giving.*
>
> *The rank next to this is of he who drops money in the Tzedakah box. One should not drop money in the box unless one is sure that the person in charge is trustworthy, wise and competent to handle the funds properly.*
>
> *The next degree to this is the person who gives alms to the needy in such a manner that the giver knows not to whom he gives and the recipient knows not from whom it is that he takes.*

Maimonides places great emphasis on anonymity. Putting money into the *Tzedakah* box insures anonymity for both the giver and the receiver. Yet, of all the acts of *Tzedakah* I can think of, in my opinion placing money into a *pushke*[45] ranks the least effective; anonymity may preserve the self-respect of the person in need, but personal contact sensitizes the giver in ways anonymity cannot match, and ultimately, makes a person more generous.

Remember the story of Iqbal Masih?[46] He came to the Broad Meadows School in Quincy, Massachusetts to speak out against child slavery. He was an 11 year old from Pakistan who had been sold into

---

[45] A *pushke* is a *Tzedakah* box.
[46] Iqbal was mentioned in Chapter 16; Ransoming Captives.

slavery for $12 when he was a small child and eventually freed by an organization dedicated to fighting child slavery.

Children are prized as slaves in many countries because they have small fingers which are perfect for the delicate work needed in weaving carpets. Iqbal spoke of his experiences to the sixth graders at the Broad Meadows School and begged the children to make sure no carpet that used children as slaves would be bought.

Iqbal returned to Pakistan where he was murdered months later. He was silenced by those who were against his crusade against child slavery. The sixth graders at Broad Meadows did not want to see Iqbal's legacy die with him. In response, they raised enough money to build a school in Iqbal's home village because they believed that education would be the key to change. The project continues and over the years other Middle School groups have paid for nurses, micro grants, and health care.[47]

Meeting Iqbal face to face reaped more benefits than any *Tzedakah* box could ever have foretold. When you know the person you are helping, a bond is formed. You become involved in their success. When you become aware of their needs you are more likely to help them in the future. A *Tzedakah* box provides no lasting *Simcha*, no lasting joy for the giver or the reviewer to build upon.

Anonymity has its place – and there are times when it is better not to know – but it also has its price. That is the point; Maimonides ladder of *Tzedakah* is not always right, and in many cases does not apply.

> *The highest degree exceeded by none is that of the person who assists a poor man by providing him with a gift or a loan or by accepting him into a business partnership or by helping him find employment – in a word, by putting him where he can dispense with other people's aid.*

According to Maimonides, the highest form of *Tzedakah* is to make

---

[47] For more information about this project; go to
www.mirrorimage.com/iqbal/index.html

it unnecessary.

Story:

A woman came to Rabbi Israel, the Maggid of Koznitz, and told him with many tears, that she had been married a dozen years and still had not borne a child.[48]

"What are you willing to do about it?" he asked her. She did not know what to say.

"My mother," so the Maggid told her, "was aging and still had no child." Then she heard that the holy Baal Shem Tov[49] *was stopping over in Apt in the course of a journey. She hurried to his inn and begged him to pray she might bear a son.*

'What are you willing to do about it?' he asked.

'My husband is a poor book-binder,' she replied, 'but I do have one fine thing that I shall give to the rabbi.'

She went home as fast as she could and fetched her good cape, her Katinka, *which was carefully stowed away in a chest. But when she returned to the inn with it, she heard that the Baal Shem had already left for Mezbizh. She immediately set out after him and since she had no money to ride, she walked from town to town with her* Katinka *until she came to Mezbizh.*

The Baal Shem took the cape and hung it on the wall.

'It is well,' he said.

My mother walked all the way back, from town to town, until she reached Apt. A year later, I was born."

"I, too," cried the woman, "will bring you a cape of mine so that I may get a son."

"That won't work," said the Maggid. "You heard the story. My mother had no story to go by." (Buber, Tales of the Hasidim, p. 286)

---

[48] In Jewish law it is considered valid grounds for divorce if a marriage has not produced a child in its first ten years.
[49] The founder of Chasidism.

Chapter 20: *Tzedakah* - Fraud

If a person comes to you for assistance, and you tell him,
"God will help you," you are acting disloyally to God.
For you should understand that God has sent you to aid
the needy person, not to refer him back to the Almighty.
(The Blue Guide to the Here & Hereafter)

We cannot solve life's problems except by solving them. That
statement may seem idiotically self evident, yet it is
seemingly beyond the comprehension of much of
the human race. (Scott Peck)

I begin this in-depth look at the *Mitzvah* of *Tzedakah* with an episode that happened to me in seminary. Why have I chosen to begin this section with an admittedly depressing story of being taken by a con artist? First, I believe that it is important that all who are involved in *Tzedakah* have their "eyes open" as to the ways of *Tzedakah* and recognize that our passion can be manipulated by the unscrupulous. Second, we need to be educated in how the *Mitzvah* can be abused for only in this way can we avoid it. Lastly, it seems that every time I tell this story or one like it, others share a time when they were "taken." We learn from common experience. There is no shame in being conned if you learn from the experience and refuse to become jaded by it.

This is the best place to start. Recognize that everyone involved in *Mitzvah* work gets taken from time to time – and that it is not a valid reason for refusing to help others. Those who stop being *Mensches* because they might be duped were never *Mensches* in the first place.

Growing up in Yeshiva one learns many stories about Elijah the Prophet.[50] *You never knew who he would be or when you would meet him, but you had to be ready.*

---

[50] According to the text Elijah never died but was carried up to heaven in a fiery chariot. He remains alive according to tradition to serve as a Divine herald and one who shows up from time to time (in disguise) to test people and teach them about ethics.

As a student I found myself standing in the Port Authority Terminal in New York City, the huge bus station that serves the city. A man walked up to me. He was dressed in a jacket and tie. He told me that he had seen my Kippah and hoped I would help him. His money was stolen and he needed $13 to buy a ticket to catch his bus to upstate New York. He knew no one in the city and had nowhere to go. Can I help him?

I didn't know what to do. But somehow, I remember all the Elijah stories. I fumble in my pockets and found my one $20 bill. Giving it to him, I said something like,

"Here take the $20 and get a meal as well."

After thanking me profusely, he took my name and address, and promised to send me the money, and left.

I have to admit, I felt good – after all, I had helped him get home. I had given him the last of my meager funds – but even the hunger felt righteous.

When, the next week, I told my older brother (who lived in the city) what I had done, he said something like,

"That's the oldest con in the book. They look for someone innocent and with that 'do gooder look' and ask them for a small sum of money. You got taken!"

Of course, I never heard from him again.

There are many people in need of *Tzedakah*. There are many more asking for it. I have learned that having good intentions and a deep pocket are not enough. One must be careful and smart as well.

For me the question was, "How do I avoid the anger that accompanies the knowledge that I was being used. How do I remain loyal to the ideals of *Tzedakah* when I see it abused?" It is comforting to learn that this is not a new problem. It has been going on for thousands of years. It seems that as long as there have been people in need, there have been people willing to pretend that they are in need.

> *Samuel in his boyhood went to sit among the poor. He overheard one say to another: "What dishes shall we use today, the golden or the silver ones?" When he told his father, Rav Abba bar Abba, he replied: "We should be thankful that there are cheats among the poor; otherwise we would have no excuse when we find it difficult to answer the plea of a poor man."*

The tradition deals with the issue in a very pragmatic fashion; there are things we are required to do and things we are not required to do. It is worthwhile to start here.

> *When a poor man says, "provide me with clothes," he should be investigated (lest he be found to be a cheat). When he says "Feed me," he should not be investigated (but fed immediately) lest he starve to death during the investigation.* (Bava Batra 9a)

In my experience most people are uncomfortable placing standards and boundaries on the *Tzedakah* they give. But we must create standards; when is *Tzedakah* required and when is it optional? When are we allowed to question and under what circumstances is it acceptable to suspect and inquire? This text is a start. We must give food on demand – all other requests may be checked. However, if someone asks for food, that is what they get. You are not required to give money for food, just the food.

I follow this standard scrupulously. My congregation is at the crossroads of several major interstates and has a bus and railway line nearby. It is well known that there are professionals who roam the interstates, contacting the houses of worship in the area and asking for $5 or $10 to get home for a meal. I found that as soon as I offered supermarket scrip[51] instead of money the three calls per week I was receiving went to zero calls per week.

---

[51] Scrip is one of the greatest inventions to the world of *Tzedakah*. The store issues paper "money" or a plastic "credit card" that can only be used in that store. Giving scrip avoids giving cash to someone who may use it for drugs or liquor.

I know that the dynamic of *Tzedakah* lends itself to dishonest people taking advantage of good-hearted donors. This situation, while deplorable, has never and will never change. Yet, we cannot allow the dishonesty of some to interfere with our responsibilities to others. The best defense is to be familiar with what our tradition teaches us about *Tzedakah* and well informed as to the appropriate responses.

> *He who is compassionate when he should be severe ends by being severe when he should be compassionate.*
> *(Kohelet Rabbah 7)*

Yet, I still look for Elijah because I believe in him. You never know when you will find him – but you will. And, when you do, it will be a life changing experience.

I have learned when and how to give and when not to give. I have learned how to offer to help each person who comes to me, imposter or real. Sometimes I offer what they will not accept: a tank of gas, a ride to the family service agency, a call home. Sometimes I buy them food or pay their bills. Sometimes I get taken – but I would rather be taken nineteen times and legitimately helping once than not help at all. I have also learned that whose who complain the loudest about the con artists are only looking for a reason not to give at all.

Home Work:

1. Look for articles in newspapers and magazines that talk about how much money is wasted in *Tzedakah* organizations or bogus charities. Discuss how it affects everyone in the community.
2. Discuss as a family how not to become cynical about giving *Tzedakah*.

Story:

The Story goes that, when the great, sweet Rabbi Zusia of Hanipol was on his deathbed, his students gathered all around him. This is what he said to them: "When I get to the Next World, I am not afraid if God will ask me,

'Zusia, why weren't you Moses, to lead the people out of this land where Jews are so oppressed and beaten by the people?"

I can answer, 'I did not have the leadership abilities of Moses.'

And if God asks, 'Zusia, why weren't you Isaiah, reprimanding the people for their sins and urging them to change their ways, to repent?'

I could answer, 'I did not have the eloquence of Isaiah, the Great Master of powerful and dazzling speech.'

No, my students, I am not afraid of those questions. What I fear is this: What if God asks me, 'Zusia, why were you Zusia?'

"Then what will I say?"

Section Three: The Holy Days, Chagim

Chapter 21: What is "Holy" about a Holiday?

"Isn't God the same everywhere?"
"He is, but I am not. (Hasidic saying)

You never know when you are making a memory.
(Ricky Lee Jones)

The word *Kadosh* means both *holy* and *separate*. The concept of *holiness* is derived from those experiences that *separate* us from the ordinary. Abraham Joshua Heschel taught that Judaism creates "holy moments in time." Some of these moments are called holy days. We can observe the yearly rituals: *Matzah* on *Passover*, *Shofar* on *Rosh Hashanah* and recognize their symbolic value yet miss the deeper meanings ascribed to them by the tradition.

Ritual was designed as a shorthand to create and reinforce meaning. We develop rituals to bring meaning into our lives. However, if the horseradish does nothing else but to remind us of the taste of Egyptian slavery we have relegated the holy day to a child's exercise in entertainment.

Each holy day is in part dedicated to the *Mitzvot* of *Tzedakah*. Each holy day has lessons to teach us about our community and gives us opportunities to relate to others in supportive ways. *Maot Chittin* on *Pesach* and *Matanot L'evyonim* on *Purim*[52] are two of the most obvious *Mitzvot*. These are holy days, not holidays. There is a difference. The term "holiday" has become a generic almost meaningless term. Labor Day is a holiday. *Passover* is a holy day.

---

[52] These *Mitzvot* will be explained in the specific holy day chapter.

Chapter 22: The High Holy Days - *Yamim Nora'im*

*If all the chastisements were placed on one scale and
poverty on the other, they would balance evenly.
(Shemot Rabbah 31:12)*

*Care less for your harvests than how it is shared, and
your life will have meaning and your heart
will have peace. (Kent Nerburn)*

We live with a practical tradition. We begin the New Year with ten days devoted to introspection. Between *Rosh Hashanah* and *Yom Kippur* we are asked to review our past; failures and victories, to evaluate our relationships and how we can make things better for ourselves and those we care for. We take stock of our lives and try to put ourselves back on the right path.

Chet, is the Hebrew word commonly translated as "sin." It is derived from the term which means "to miss the target." The assumption is that sin is a mistake; an action we would correct if possible. It is human to make mistakes – it is brave to try to correct them. This makes *Teshuvah*, translated as "to return" an attainable task. We are not expected to be perfect but we are expected to clean up the messes we have made.

Our Covenant divides our relationships into two categories: those we have with each other and the relationship we have with God. The mistakes we make fall into these categories as well:

1. The ways in which we hurt others and
2. The ways in which we hurt God.

Isn't it incredible that we can hurt God? Some may disagree and ask "How can a perfect God be concerned with our sins?" In my opinion it is a measure of God's love for us that God created a relationship in which God is affected by our actions. And, while some may say this is only a metaphor – I am not so sure. If one truly believes in the concept of *Tikun Olam* and recognizes our responsibility to fix the world, how can God not be disappointed and hurt when we fail?

This interplay between *Teshuvah* and *Chet*, our relationship to God and our relationship to others creates a very involved dynamic and ideally forces us to face our frailties and responsibilities. We have made mistakes – how can we atone for them?

> *On Yom Kippur we are required to give a ransom for our lives, for it is at this time that all people are counted and pass before (God). Thus, it is the custom to give Tzedakah on Yom Kippur.*
> *(Ba'al Haturim on Exodus 30)*

A customary ritual performed before *Yom Kippur* is called, *Kapparot*. This ritual involves a person taking a sum of money (or a live chicken), grasping it in his hand and as he circles his head with the object recites that this will be my **substitute** and shall be given to *Tzedakah* by me. The chicken is then donated to poor people or the money is given to *Tzedakah*. In this way *Tzedakah* is used to avert the evil decree.

The word "ransom" is used because God holds our lives in hand. In order to be freed of the evil decree we must pay for it. The ransom is used as *Tzedakah* and in a real way we live the phrase, "*Tzedakah* saves from death."

> *Rav Yuden said in the name of Rav Eliezer, "Three things invalidate evil decrees, they are Prayer, Tzedakah and Teshuvah."*
> *(Kohelet Rabbah 5:4)*

This is one of the more familiar texts from the High Holy Day liturgy. Whether you believe it or not it is important to recognize that it is a foundation of belief in our tradition.

We find an interesting disagreement in Rabbinic literature concerning prayer and *Tzedakah*:

> *The students of Rabbi Akiva asked him, "Which is greater, Teshuvah or Tzedakah?"*
> *He answered them, "Teshuvah, because sometimes one gives Tzedakah to one who does not need it. However, Teshuvah comes from within (is always needed)."*
> *They (the students) said to him, "Rabbi, have we not already found that Tzedakah is greater than Teshuvah, with Abraham and (king) David?"*   (Midrash Mishle 6:6)

In this text Rabbi *Akiva* places emphasis on the necessity of *Teshuvah*. We are always in need of repentance and atonement. Yet the students refuse to accept this answer. The text does not resolve the matter and seemingly leaves the matter for us to decide. I believe this text identifies one of the most important issues in our community today.

How does one explore Judaism and derive deep meaning from it? What if you want to strengthen your Jewish identity? One way is to become introspective and find yourself in the intense moments we create through silent ritual and prayer. This is the essence of *Teshuvah*, the "return" to ones tradition. We look for God in these moments of prayer and study, wrapped in a *Tallit* and speaking to the Divine. This is one way, and it is a good way. But it is not the only way.

Another way to achieve this goal is to immerse oneself in *Tzedakah*. I have experienced moments of spiritual delight, wrapped in my *Tallit* and turning towards God, when the door opened and my path was illuminated. But I have also experienced the intensity of giving a bag of school supplies to a child who has never had them before, or delivering 20,000 pounds of food to a shelter in Mississippi that was on the verge of closing for lack of supplies. I can tell you this: when I am alone and feel in the dark, scared and aware of my mortality, when I am in pain, it is the *Tzedakah* experiences I dust-off and recall. They bring me back. When I am depressed it is going out and helping a person in need that brings me out of depression. For me, prayer and ritual are vital expressions of my identity and form the basis of my observance – but my humanity comes from *Tzedakah*.

> *And this is also an answer to poor people who say, "How can we do good things? We have nothing to which to give to the poor?"*
> *These words are without value, for it is possible to give Tzedakah by doing good deeds and by keeping the Mitzvot...Is there greater Tzedakah than this? Even a poor person should give a little Tzedakah, even if he is (solely) supported from Tzedakah...For the little from him is as important as much from a rich person.*
> (Orchot Tzadikim 8)

Home Work:

1. List all the holy days and holidays that you celebrate (including birthdays, anniversaries, etc.) Connect *Tzedakah* organizations that are particularly appropriate to each event (e.g. Battered Women's shelter--Mother's Day, Birthday Angels for birthdays). Donate to that organization on the appropriate day.
2. Do *Kapparot*. Use money (not the chicken). Donate the money to *Tzedakah*. Discuss why the tradition would teach that *Tzedakah* can avert an evil decree.
3. See if there are any college students in the area, or singles (of any age) that need home hospitality for *Rosh Hashanah* or *Yom Kippur*.
4. How does your congregation allocate High Holy Day tickets to guests and non members – see how your congregation could be more hospitable to them.
5. Read the Story If Not Higher, by I.L. Peretz.

<u>Stories:</u>

Rabbi Yochanan ben Zakkai was one day going out of Jerusalem, accompanied by his disciple, Rabbi Yehoshua. At the time the Temple was in ruins.

Yehoshua said, "Woe, the place where the iniquities were atoned for is destroyed."

Rabbi Yochanan replied, "Do not grieve. We have an atonement which is equally good, namely deeds of mercy, the charity that has a personal character."

(Avot D'Rabi Natan 4,5)

Rabbi Israel Salanter, one of the most distinguished Orthodox Rabbis of the nineteenth century, failed to appear one Yom Kippur eve to chant the sacred Kol Nidre Prayer. His congregation became concerned, for it was inconceivable that their saintly rabbi would be late or absent on this very holy day. They sent out a search party to look for him. After much time, their rabbi was found in the barn of a Christian neighbor. On his way to the synagogue, Rabbi Salanter had come upon one of his neighbor's calves, lost and tangled in the brush. Seeing that the animal was in distress, he freed it and led it home through many fields and over many hills. His act of mercy represented the rabbi's prayers on that Yom Kippur evening.

(Jewish Virtual Library as told by Richard Schwartz)

Chapter 23: *Sukkot*:

Just as one cannot fulfill his duty on Sukkot unless all "four species" are held together, by the same token Israel cannot be redeemed unless all Israelites hold together.
(Yalkut 188a)

Finding meaning does not require us to live differently, it requires us to see our lives differently.
(Rachel Remen)

The two most important *Mitzvot* associated with the holy day of Sukkot are that of building a *Sukkah* and using the "four species:" *Lulav* (palm branch), *Etrog* (citron), *Hadas* (willow) and *Aravot* (myrtle). One of the most enjoyable experiences of the year for me is eating a meal in a homemade *Sukkah*[53] One custom performed each night before dinner in the *Sukkah* is called *Ushpizin*. The *Ushpizin* are historical guests we invite to dine with us. Traditionally, the *Ushpizin* are Abraham, Isaac, Jacob, Joseph, Moses, Aaron and David.[54]

In a very real sense, *Sukkot* is about hospitality. We not only invite guests to join us at the meal, we invite our history as well. We celebrate the concept of community.

---

[53] Not a prefab Sukkah, one that is built with hammer and nails. It never looks pretty. No one has ever accused me of having carpenter genes – but it is enjoyable nonetheless.
[54] Although I favor a newer custom of deciding whom the family would like to invite with them: a deceased ancestor, a not yet born great grandchild or any other figure in history or literature, fictional or real.

> *The Etrog has a fragrance and a taste symbolic of those in Israel who possess an abundance of Torah and Mitzvah.*
> *The Lulav has no fragrance, but has taste, symbolic of those scholars who perform only a few kind deeds.*
> *The myrtle has a fragrance, but no taste, symbolic of kindly persons who are unlearned.*
> *The willow has neither taste or fragrance, symbolic of those who are neither learned, nor kind.*
> *God says, "It is impossible for Me to destroy them, but let them all be united, and let each atone for the other."*
> *(Yalkut Shimoni: Emor)*

It is significant that when performing the *Mitzvah*, all four species must be held in contact with each other. Each person contributes to the whole and everyone is related.

Home Work:

1. Build a Sukkah. Make plans to eat at least one meal there. Discuss who you would invite to your meal with the family.
2. Decorate your Sukkah with gloves, hats and mittens (sealed in clean plastic bags), as a reminder of our exposure to the elements. After Sukkot, donate the collection to a local organization.
3. Learn about the agricultural laws of "corners" and "gleanings." Then set apart a corner of a cupboard to collect food items for donation and your personal "gleanings" (the things you have left behind on your closet's shelves), so that others may enjoy them.
4. Locate a local family farm and take your family to gather part of the fall harvest or inquire about gleaning at the farm. Distribute what you have collected to a local soup kitchen or shelter. If you are fortunate enough to grow your own home garden, be sure to harvest every last crop (even if you just *cannot* bake one more zucchini bread) and visit the website www.ampleharvest.org to locate nearby shelters or pantries

that can use your product.

Story:

Jewish law ordains that Jews acquire an etrog before the holiday of Sukkot, and recite a blessing over it each day of the festival (except on Shabbat).

The Nobel Prize laureate and novelist, S.Y. Agnon relates the following story:

In his Jerusalem neighborhood, shortly before Sukkot, he ran into one of his neighbors, an elderly rabbi from Russia, at a store selling etrogim. The rabbi told him that since Jewish law regards it as uniquely special to acquire a very beautiful etrog, he was willing to spend a large sum to acquire this ritual object, notwithstanding his limited means.

Agnon was surprised, a day later, when the holiday began and the rabbi did not take out his etrog during the synagogue service. Perplexed, he asked the man where the beautiful etrog was.

The rabbi told him the following story:

I awoke early, as is my habit, and prepared to recite the blessing over the etrog in my Sukkah on my balcony. My neighbor with a large family has a balcony adjoining mine. The father of all these children is unfortunately a man of short temper...As I stood in the sukkah on my balcony...I heard a child weeping...one of the children of our neighbor. I walked over to find out what was wrong. She told me she too had awakened early and had gone out on her balcony to examine her father's etrog...Against her father's instructions, she removed the etrog from its protective box...dropped the etrog on the stone floor, irreparably damaging it...I comforted her, and I then took my etrog and placed it in her father's box, taking the damaged etrog to my premises. I told her to tell her father that his neighbor insisted that he accept the gift of his etrog and that he would be honoring me and the holiday by so doing...

Agnon concluded: "My rabbinic neighbor's damaged, bruised, ritually unusable etrog was the most beautiful etrog I have ever seen in my lifetime."

(As told by Dov Greenberg)

Chapter 24: *Chanukah*

Heaven forbid we should ever abandon the law and its statutes. We will not obey the command of the king, nor will we deviate one step from our form of worship. (Mattathias, I Maccabees, 2:1ff)

God's Menorah is even more beautiful (than a Chanukah Menorah), God's Menorah is made of people, not of candles. (Rachel Naomi Remen)

If there was ever a Holy Day made for Hollywood it's *Chanukah*. The few fought the many, the weak overcame the strong. The fight for religious freedom rang. And, like so many other Hollywood stories, what we have been taught is that the tale is not that close to the truth! The texts of *Chanukah* tell a somewhat different story. *Chanukah* started as a civil war between rival factions trying to control the office of the High Priest (the *Kohen Gadol*). There were the assimilationists versus the traditionalists. The assimilationists called for help from the Syrian-Greeks. They came and stayed. What had started as a localized civil conflict became a full fledged war.

We read about the turning point in the conflict from the book of I Maccabees:

> *The king's officers who were enforcing apostasy came to the town of Modin to see that sacrifice was offered. Many Jews went over to them. Mattathias and his sons stood in a group. The king's officers spoke to Mattathias:*
>
> *"You are a leader here...You be the first now to come forward and carry out the king's order. All the nations have done so..."*
>
> *Mattathias replied in a ringing voice..."We will not obey the command of the king nor will we deviate one step from our own worship."*
>
> *As soon as he had finished, a Jew stepped forward in full view of all to offer sacrifice on the pagan altar at Modin, in obedience to the royal command...Mattathias rushed forward and killed the traitor at the very altar. At the same time he killed the officer sent by the king to enforce sacrifice, and pulled down the altar...He and his sons took to the hills, leaving all their belongings behind in the town.*
>
> (I Maccabees, 2:15 - 28)

Chanukah is a holy day that personifies the *Mitzvah* of *Al Ta'amod, Do Not Stand Idly By*. As the forces of Antiochus perpetrated atrocities and abomination upon Judaism – Mattathias and his son Judah kept the flame alive.

This is not to say that the Maccabees were not as heroic as they are portrayed in our classrooms and pulpits, or as successful as we would want to believe. Judah did capture and cleanse the Temple in Jerusalem. He did not hold it forever though. Eventually he was killed in battle. The Hasmonean dynasty founded by the Maccabees ended up more assimilated than those they originally fought. They were not perfect. However, at the right time and in the right place their accomplishments are undiminished.

Chanukah retains its theme of *Do Not Stand Idly By* in modern times too. I grew up in a small town community. *Chanukah* was a time when religious freedom was tested by those who would seek to display religious symbols on public property. When I was one of five rabbis who were imprisoned by the United States government for protesting the treatment of Soviet Jews, we were imprisoned on *Chanukah*[55] and were nicknamed "The Maccabee Five."

The following year, when I was sent to the former Soviet Union to visit Refuseniks[56] I found that *Chanukah* was an important Holy Day for them. Religious freedom was a precious commodity to them. They would make a *Chanukah Menorah* by cutting a potato in two, hollowing out a depression in one half and placing a candle in it. That way, if the KGB or a neighbor called they could quickly dispose of the evidence.

There were no greater models for the *Mitzvah* of *Al Ta'amod* than the Refuseniks of the Soviet Union.

Home Work:

1. Everyone gets gifts for Chanukah. Choose one gift that will be given to *Tzedakah*.
2. Learn how to play Dreidel. At the beginning of every pot, have each player place one penny into a *Tzedakah* box. Let the winner decide to which *Tzedakah* project the money will go.

Story:

Julie Leirich stole food from the supermarket that employed her. Leirich was working as a supermarket checker in a large grocery store in Los Angeles. She couldn't bear it when she saw how much perfectly good food was removed from the market's shelves and showcases, and thrown into a dumpster. Leirich knew that there were thousands of hungry people in the city, and here was all this food being wasted.

Leirich began "intercepting" food headed for the dumpster, sneaking it out of the market, and giving it to hungry people on the streets. The people were grateful, but Leirich felt guilty; she finally told her boss she'd been taking the food.

To her surprise and relief, he didn't fire her – he offered her more food to take to the street people.

Now that her efforts were "legal," Leirich started an organization called

---

[55] And released Christmas Eve.
[56] Those Soviet Jews who had applied for visas to emigrate and been "refused."

"The Loving Cup" and asked the customers in her check-out line to contribute. Then she went to other markets and to restaurants, getting them to give food too. Within months, Julie Leirich's Loving Cup was "rescuing" over six tons of food a month for the poor of Los Angeles.

Chapter 25: *Purim*

If there be no Israel in the world...there will be no Torah.
(Midrash Panim Aherim)

It is hard not to see the person you are helping as someone weaker than yourself, someone more needy...but we do not serve with our strength, we serve with ourselves. (Rachel Naomi Remen)

The merriment, costumes and carnivals with which we celebrate *Purim* lead many to believe that *Purim* is a children's Holy Day. While it is true that these customs are meant to engage the child in all of us there is a serious side to this day, one that is often hidden by the noise of drowning out *Haman's* name.

There are four *Mitzvot* to be observed on Purim:

1. To hear the *Megillah*, the story of *Purim*, read.
2. To send gifts of food (*Mishloach Manot*) to friends.
3. To take part in a special *Purim* meal (*Seudah*).
4. To give presents to the poor (*Matanot La'evyonim*)

The last two *Mitzvot*, the *Purim Seudah* and *Matanot La'evyonim*, have special meaning for us. The *Mitzvah* of *Matanot La'evyonim* comes directly from the *Megillah* of *Esther*.

> *Mordechai recorded these events. He sent dispatches to all the Jews throughout the provinces of King Achasverosh, near and far, charging them to observe the fourteenth and fifteenth days of Adar, every year. The same days on which the Jews enjoyed relief from their foes and the same month which had been transformed for them from one of grief and mourning to one of festive merrymaking, and as an occasion for sending Mishloach Manot and Matanot La'evyonim.*
> *(Esther 9:20-23)*

It is not enough that we recognize the transition from "grief and mourning to festive merrymaking." All the members of our community must celebrate because the entire community was saved. It thus becomes required of us to make sure everyone can share in the celebration.

> *One should spend more money on gifts to the poor than on his Purim Seudah and Mishloach Manot. No joy is greater and more glorious than the joy of gladdening the hearts of the poor, the orphans, the widows and the strangers.*
> *(Maimonides, Laws of Megillah 2:18)*

And the tradition specifically notes that money given to the poor for *Purim* is not the same as *Tzedakah*.

> *Monies that are set aside to be divided among the poor for the Purim Seudah may not be used for other purposes.*
> *(Mishnah Berurah, Laws of Megillah 694:2)*

We learned that the *Mitzvah* of *Tzedakah* is so great that it can "avert the evil decree" (see High Holy Days). There the liturgy talks about health and life. There are other forms of evil decree; the inability to be part of a communal celebration is especially hard on *Purim*, when everyone is happy. It is hard to see everyone celebrating when you have nothing to celebrate. Perhaps that is the reason why funds reserved for Purim celebration cannot be distributed as *Tzedakah*.

> *It was told concerning Rabbi Chaninah ben Teradyon, one time the funds (for the poor) for Purim became (by mistake) interchanged with the funds for Tzedakah. He sat, stunned, and said,*
> *"Woe is me, for I deserve to die..."*
> *(Masechet Kallah)*

We must dedicate funds for *Purim* observance. The tradition though recognizes that celebrating *Purim* may not be a high priority to a poor person.

> *However, the poor person (who received the money) has permission to use it for other needs.*
> *(Mishnah Berurah, Laws of Megillah 694:9)*

Which leads us to an important ethical lesson: Once money is given to a poor person, it is theirs. They can use it for whatever **they** wish. This is one of the reasons the tradition requires us to give food when asked but not money. Once the money is in his possession, he is allowed to determine his own priorities.

Home Work:

1. Read Lesson 13 in *Forty Things You Can Do to Save the Jewish People*, by Joel Grishaver. Follow the directions there.
2. Collect money for *Matanot La'evyonim*. Discuss with your family where it should go. Make sure it is donated to the appropriate agency on Purim.
3. Create packages of *Mishloach Manot* and deliver them to local group homes, hospitals or to someone in your community who might be alone.
4. Do an internet search for organizations that provide Purim funds.

Story:

Having just given the beggar money for food, the man saw him not ten minutes later in a restaurant eating a bagel and lox. He confronted the beggar. "Why are you buying such an expensive meal with the money I gave you? Don't you know you could have eaten for a whole day with that money?"

The beggar sighed, "You know, I don't have enough money to eat a bagel and lox. And when you give me money you don't want me to eat a bagel with lox. So tell me mister, when can I eat a bagel and lox?"

Chapter 26: *Pesach*

It is forbidden to give up hope
(Yuli Kasharovsky)[57]

The central ritual of *Passover*, the *Seder*, takes place at home. The introductory statement of the *Haggadah* which begins the *Seder* is the *Ha Lachma Anya*:

> *This is the bread of affliction (Lechem Oni)*
> *Our ancestors ate in the land of Egypt.*
> *Let all who are hungry come in and eat.*
> *Let all who are in need, come in and share the Pesach (sacrifice).*
> *This year we are slaves,*
> *Next year, we will be free.*
> *This year, we are here.*
> *Next year, we will be in Jerusalem.*

This introduction to the *Seder* is written in Aramaic, not Hebrew. This is significant because at the time of the *Seder*, Hebrew was not the spoken language of the Jews – Aramaic was. When the rabbis wanted to make sure that the participants of a service understood what they were reading they left it in Aramaic.[58] The rabbis wanted to be certain that the message of the Ha Lachma Anya was understood.

---

[57] I met Yuli in the former Soviet Union while he was still a Refusenik. In his apartment, with hidden KGB microphones throughout the apartment, his wife observed that they would never be given permission to leave the Soviet Union. Yuli firmly stated, "It is forbidden for Jews to give up hope, even if we never get out of here, we are still not allowed to lose hope." It was gratifying to know that within four years of that statement Yuli was able to emigrate to Israel.

[58] The only other part of the *Seder* that is in Aramaic is the *Chad Gadya*, which ends the *Seder*. Other examples of Aramaic prayers are the *Kaddish* (including the Mourners Kaddish) and *Kol Nidre*.

> *It is remembered that Matzah is "Lechem Oni." This is to say that we are commanded to remember that we went out wanting, that is as poor people. We were in Egypt, eating poor bread and water.*
> *(Ramban Deuteronomy 17)*

It is a humbling experience to know that your ancestors were "the poorest" in the world. Slavery is our origin, which is why we have a responsibility not to forget and be sensitive to others. So the *Passover* celebration is a strong reminder of our obligation to help others in the same situation – because in the beginning we ourselves needed *Tzedakah*.

One observance of the *Mitzvah* of *Passover* involves the giving of *Maot Chittim* (wheat money). These are funds donated to poor people so that they can celebrate *Pesach* correctly.

The second important *Mitzvah* associated with *Pesach* deals with ransoming captives. We are reminded in the *Torah* several times that we were "strangers" in the land of Egypt. God redeemed us and made a Covenant with us. But we were not the only ones redeemed from Egypt.

> *Rabbi Meir said, "Not only Israel, but God also was redeemed at the Exodus, as it is written, 'whom you did redeem to you out of Egypt, the nation and his God.'"   (Shemot Rabbah 12:2)*

When we learn about our Covenantal relationship with God we find that our God is One who experiences history with us. We were slaves with God in Egypt. Similarly, when we feed the hungry, we are feeding God. When we clothe the naked, we are dressing God. When we perform a *Mitzvah* of any kind, God is acting with us.

Home Work:

1. Read the story on page 69 in <u>Jewish Stories One Generation Tells Another</u>, entitled, "The Boiled Eggs" and compare it to the *Mitzvot* of *Passover*.
2. Read the story entitled, "The Reminder" in <u>Who Knows</u>

Ten? Why is this story appropriate to *Passover*?
3. Hold a *Passover* food drive. Collect food that is *Kosher* for *Passover* and take it to a *Kosher* Food Pantry.
4. Collect money for *Maot Chittin*. Donate it to a social service agency that will distribute it to poor people.
5. Add a symbol to your Seder table that demonstrates your new understanding of *Passover*.

Story:

A poor man came to Rabbi Yosef Soloveichik's house. The man said that he had come to ask a question regarding the sacred rituals of Passover. He told the rabbi that he could not afford to buy wine, so he wished to know if he could fulfill the obligation to drink four cups of wine during the seder by drinking four cups of milk. Rabbi Yosef said that no Jew could fulfill this important religious commandment with milk. The rabbi then gave the man twenty five rubles with which to buy wine.

After the man had gone, the Rabbi's wife went to her husband with a question. Why, when wine cost two or three rubles, had the rabbi given the man twenty five?

Rabbi Yosef smiled and said, "When a poor Jew asks if he can use milk at his seder because he cannot afford wine, it is obvious that he cannot afford meat either. (Epstein 217)

Chapter 27: *Shavuot*

The Torah was not given to angels.
(Berakhot 25)

Life breaks us all, but afterwards, many of us
are strongest at the broken places.
(Ernest Hemingway)

Shavuot suffers from bad timing; it occurs fifty days after the beginning of *Passover,* a time when religious schools are closed for the year. The *Megillah* of Ruth is read on *Shavuot* because it details the story of Ruth who is considered the model convert to Judaism. Naomi had two sons who married Ruth and Orpah. The son's marriages bore no children. After Naomi's husband and two sons died she wishes to return to the land of Israel without her daughters in law. She urges her daughters in law to return to their own families.

> *Naomi said to her two daughters in law.*
> *"Go, and return each of you to her mother's house and may God do chesed with you just as you have done with the dead and with me...turn back my daughters. Why are you going with me? Do I have any more sons in my womb who could be your husbands?...Go! For I am too old to have a husband." But Ruth said, "Don't urge me to leave you, not to go back with you. For wherever you go I will go. Where you lodge I will lodge. Your people are my people, your God is my God. Where you die I will die and there I will be buried. Thus may God do to me, and more, for only death will separate us."*
> *(Ruth 1:8 - 17)*

In the ancient world an elderly widow without male children is powerless. Ruth's desire to share Naomi's fate shows her character; she will not desert her elderly mother in law. When they return to Israel it is Ruth who works to keep them both fed.

> *Ruth the Moabite said to Naomi,*
> *"I will go to a field and I will glean among the ears of grain behind someone who seems nice."* (Ruth 2:2)

In the Torah farmers are required to leave part of their harvest for the poor. In particular, if the workers drop any stalks of grain as they are harvesting, they are not allowed to pick them up. They are left on the ground for the poor to glean. Gleaning was hard work and the gleaners were not always treated with respect. Ruth finds herself in the field of a man named Boaz, who, we later find, is a relative of Naomi.

> *So she (Ruth) went and she came and gleaned in the field behind the harvesters. It happened that she came upon the field belonging to Boaz...He said to his harvesters, ...*
> *"to whom does that young woman belong?"*
> *The servants answered, "That is the Moabite woman who returned with Naomi from the fields of Moab..."*
> *Boaz said to Ruth, "Hear me my daughter, do not go to glean in another field. Don't leave here. Stay with my maidens. Keep your eyes on the field where they are harvesting and go after them...If you are thirsty go to the jugs and drink from the water the young men have drawn."*
> *She fell on her face and bowed to the ground and said to him, "Why have I found favor in your eyes that you are paying attention to me when I am a foreigner?"*
> *Boaz answered... "It has been told to me what you did with your mother in law after the death of your husband...May God reward your actions and may your payment be full from the Lord God under whose wings you have come for refuge."*
> *She told her mother in law where she had worked and with whom. She told her the name of the man by whom she worked was Boaz. Naomi said to her daughter in law,*
> *"Blessed is he to God who has not left his Chesed of the living and of the dead."* (Ruth 2:3 - 11)

Boaz returns favor for favor. What Ruth did for Naomi, Boaz does for Ruth. *Shavuot* is the holiday that celebrates the revelation at Sinai. Ruth embodies the faith and spirit of the *Torah* we received. Faith and action are the model we follow.

Boaz and Ruth will marry and give birth to a son who is the grandfather of King David. The text suggests that if Ruth had not followed Naomi back to Israel, had she not shown Naomi kindness and loyalty she would never have met Boaz. Had Boaz and Ruth never met King David would never have been born. *Tzedakah* brought them together.

The story of Ruth brings up another question; was it just coincidence that Ruth went to glean in the field of Boaz, or was it the hand of God? The older I get the less I believe in coincidence. I believe our lives are composed of threads of "coincidence" where we intersect with other lives and circumstances. Each life we touch, each circumstance we encounter gives us the chance to bring about some form of *Tikun Olam*. This weaving is a constant in our lives – if we allow ourselves to be sensitive to it. Ruth and Boaz "met" because of the *Mitzvot* they performed – and their union gave birth to King David.

Home Work:

1. Check the local papers and internet news for any story that refers to someone performing an act of *Chesed*.
2. Look at each of the Ten Commandments. Match a *Mitzvah* in this book to each commandment. Create a plan and a *Mitzvah* project based upon the matching of these *Mitzvot*.
3. As a family discussion, debate which value is more important, learning *Torah* or doing *Tzedakah*.
4. Plant a portion of your family's garden specifically for vegetables and fruits that will be donated to a soup kitchen or shelter. Go to www.AmpleHarvest.org to learn where local food pantries may be located in your community. If you know of a local food pantry that is not registered, urge them to register on AmpleHarvest.org so others (locally) who grow a fruit/vegetable garden can learn where they may bring their own produce.

Story:

There is also a story about two brothers that explains why the Holy Temple was built where it was built. Here is the story: Many years ago, there were two brothers that loved each other very much. They lived close one to the other. It was the period of collecting the produces from the fields. They both had the same amount of wheat. One of the brothers was married and had children, but the other one lived alone and had no wife and children. One night, the lonely brother woke up and thought: "My brother has a wife and children and they all have to eat but I am only one person and I don't need so much wheat, I will give him some of my wheat." He got up and put some wheat from his pile to the pile of his brother. At the same night, the other brother woke up and thought: 'my brother lives alone, he has no wife and children. I am happy with my family but he has no family. I will give him some of my wheat so he will be more happy.' He woke up and put in his brother's pile of wheat, some wheat from his pile.

In the morning, they were very surprised to see that the both piles are equal but they said nothing. It happened again the night after and in the third night, they woke up in the same time, and they met. They were so surprised to see each other!!! They said something like 'what are you doing here'. But then they understood what happened and they hugged and kissed each other. God saw the big love of the brothers, and some years later, in the same place, the Holy Temple was built!

Chapter 28: *Shabbat*

In two ways does man lend to God: in donating to the needy and in spending money for the Shabbat and Festivals.   (Zohar II 255a)

A right is not what someone gives you: It's what no one can take from you.   (Ramsey Clark)

Shabbat is the holiest day of the year.[59] The best description I have ever read of *Shabbat* comes from Harold Kushner. We come to a fascinating Talmudic text:

> *I suspect that a lot of us were taught about Shabbat in terms of keeping some arbitrary rules in order to please God. But that's not what it's really about. It's about the process of reclaiming your soul. Traditional Jews don't spend money on Shabbat. They don't go to the office or the shopping mall because money is the symbol of the economic war we are engaged in six days a week – a war which teaches us to see our fellow human beings as competitors, and that point of view shrinks our soul. Shabbat, when you do it right, is a day when individuals stop running on their individual schedules and define themselves as a Jewish family, as people who belong to each other in a permanent, intimate way.*

We come to a fascinating Talmudic text:

> *Rabbi Akiva said the following to his son Joshua: Make your Shabbat as a week-day rather than depend for support upon other people.*
> *(Pesachim 112a)*

This is a not-so-subtle message. It is better to "make *Shabbat* as a weekday," to work on *Shabbat*, than to keep *Shabbat* by accepting

---

[59] *Yom Kippur* is actually the holiest day of the year. However, this is by virtue of the fact that it is called "*Shabbat Shabbaton*," the "Sabbath of Sabbaths" in the *Torah*.

Tzedakah..[60] We learn in the tradition that *Shabbat* may be broken to save a life. Rabbi Akiva expands the category.

I find this text so meaningful because it is descriptive of the immigrant experience. My grandfather came to this country as a Jew who was a Sabbath observer. The United States at that time was the *Goldineh Medinah*, the "golden land." Religious freedom meant that Jews could enter any occupation or business. There were obstacles and there was anti-Semitism, but compared to the Europe he had left, this was truly the land of opportunity.

The opportunity came at a price though. He could work – but he could not find a job and have *Shabbat* too. His choice was to either be unemployed and destitute with *Shabbat* or poor without it. He made the decision to leave *Shabbat* behind. He did what he could – but eventually lost the observance completely.

To me he made the right decision. I doubt he was happy with it and I suppose it tore his heart out – but for him it was better than having *Shabbat* because of *Tzedakah*.

Home Work:

1. Light candles for *Shabbat*. Before you light candles, put money into the *Tzedakah* box. Make it a family decision as to where the money should be donated.
2. Buy *Challahs* for *Shabbat*. Buy extra and bring to shut ins or poor people you know. Help someone else celebrate *Shabbat*.
3. Invite other families to share *Shabbat* dinners with you.
4. Make sure that some portion of the *Shabbat* meal is dedicated to a discussion on *Tikun Olam*.

Story:

There was once a wealthy but miserly man who lived in the days of King

---

[60] I must point out that Akiva's teaching is not found in the Legal codes. According to current Jewish law it is better to accept *Tzedakah* than break *Shabbat*. However Akiva's text is the starting point of an interesting values-discussion.

Solomon. Many people attempted to make him sensitive to people in need. He would not listen. Finally, King Solomon heard about him – and decided to teach him a lesson.

One day, the man opened his door to see the King's carriage in front of his home. The King's own Prime Minister had come to hand deliver a personal invitation to have Shabbat dinner with the King. The man was so very flattered and bragged to everyone who would listen (and many who would not) that he had been singled out by the King for a special dinner.

So miserly was the man that, in anticipation of the meal he did not eat for almost two days before. He was going to enjoy the meal.
Friday came and the man, hungry as he had never been before, came into the palace for the dinner. He was met by the King's chief butler who gave him the following instructions:

First; you are not allowed to begin eating your course until the King finishes his food. Second: no matter what the King asks, you must smile and never complain. Third; always compliment the food.

With that, the man was whisked into the King's presence. It was exactly as he had been told, the dinner was just for King Solomon and him.

The first course was fish. It looked and smelled delicious. The King took his time eating all the while having the man tell him of his life. When the King was done, no sooner had the man picked up his fork to eat his fish then the servants cleared the table!

The next course was soup. The king took his time eating. The man, so very hungry by now, could hardly wait for the king to finish his soup. However, as soon as the king was finished with his soup, the servants cleared the table!

So it was with each course. The man never got a chance to eat. But, he had to compliment the king and the food at the end of each course.

At the end of the hours-long meal, the king asked the man if he had enjoyed his meal. The man had to say "yes."

"Isn't it interesting" remarked King Solomon, "How hard it is to sit at a table of plenty and go hungry? It is almost as hard for me to see a man with so much give nothing to the many who need it."

The man got the message – and became someone who welcomed those who were hungry at his own table.

Chapter 29: In Conclusion

*When people look at others with an open heart, the
connection they experience makes it a simpler thing to
forgive, to have compassion, to serve and to love...
Perhaps the healing of the world rests on just this sort
of shift in our way of seeing...*   (Rachel Naomi Remen)

We often talk about the "chain of Jewish tradition." This is more than just a pretty phrase. It is an accurate description of the values and strengths of our community. Interconnected links support each other. Put enough of these links together and you have an unbreakable line that connects any two points. Each of us is a link in this chain. Put enough of us together and you have an unbreakable tradition that reaches from our past to our future. But how do we insure that our links remain interconnected? How do we effectively communicate our values from one generation to another?

Doing *Mitzvah* is not enough. We must actively model for the next generation. We must be aware that every moment, every action has the potential to create memories for those we love. Creating memories forms stories. Stories connect the links.

Each of us is the main character in the story of our lives. We share ourselves with others by telling our narratives and it is through narratives that we often learn the greatest lessons. We live within the framework of tales about success and failure or good and evil. Our self perception is seen through these accounts.

There is a reason that the *Torah* begins with stories. The entire book of Genesis and the first half of the book of Exodus tells the story of our people. These texts have a power that transcends time and history.

There is a story that is told about a Prince who thought he was a rooster. The King and Queen tried every remedy available but they could not convince him that he was really a human being. After many weeks a Rabbi came forward and promised a remedy. He introduced himself to the Prince as a fellow rooster and lived with the Prince for two weeks.

After two weeks he asked the Prince, "Why are we sleeping on the floor."

The Prince replied, "That is what roosters do."

The Rabbi asked, "Just because we are roosters we can still sleep in beds." So they began sleeping in beds.

You can guess the rest of the story. Eventually the Rabbi had the Prince eating, sleeping and talking just like a human being. As the Prince was about to resume his responsibilities, he turned to the Rabbi and asked, "How can I be a Prince when I know inside that I am just a rooster?"

The Rabbi replied, "Just because you are a rooster doesn't mean you can't act like a prince."

This story is the story of our people. No matter what we think of ourselves, it is what we do that determines who we are. And each person's potential is unlimited. Look at our models; Moses had a speech defect and the Patriarchs had dysfunctional families. Some of the greatest Rabbis in the Talmud were blind and deformed. We can achieve great heights.

The greatest act of *Tzedakah* I ever witnessed was performed by a person with Borderline Personality Disorder. I can only hope that my place in heaven is close to him, because I can never approach his level of giving. I, have never given all I had to *Tzedakah*.

These beliefs are a great and awesome beauty within our tradition. Despite being mistake-prone human beings we can fly on angel's wings. All we have to do is take that first step, and the next step after.

This work has its rewards. Performing *Mitzvot* gives a person self-worth and grounds them in values. It provides light in times of darkness and heals the wounds life gives us.

I can promise you this; no one who busied themselves performing the *Mitzvot* described in this book ever died alone or without friends. There is a saying in our tradition, *Mitzvah Goreret Mitzvah,* one *Mitzvah* leads to another. This is a fact of life – and can be a fact in each of our lives as well.

Blessed is the Lord our God, who has kept me alive and alert, allowing me to reach this day.

Appendix I
Maimonides Description of *Lashon Harah*

Text	Commentary
Whoever acts like a **spy** against his neighbor violates a Negative *Mitzvah*, for it is written "You shall not go about spreading slander among your people." **(Leviticus 19:16)**...It is a flagrant offense which has brought about the **death** of many Jewish individuals. Who is a talebearer? One who carries gossip, going about from person to person and telling: "So and so said this: I have heard so and so about so and so." Even though he tells the truth, he **ruins the world**. There is still worse iniquity that comes with this prohibition, namely; the evil tongue of the scandalmonger who speaks disparagingly of his fellow man, even if he tells **the truth**. But the one who disparages his neighbor by telling a lie is called a slanderer. It makes no difference whether a man deals out gossip in the presence or the absence of the party concerned. Anyone who tells things that, if transmitted from person to person, are likely to cause physical or financial harm to a fellow man, or merely to distress or frighten him, is guilty of slander. All these scandalmongers in whose neighborhood it is forbidden to live; it is all the more forbidden to be in their company and **hear their talk**. The sentence was confirmed and sealed against our forefathers **in the wilderness** only for slandering...He who takes revenge violates a Negative *Mitzvah*...One should rather be forbearing with regard to all worldly things, which, in the opinion of the wise, are **sheer vanity** and nothingness; they are not worthy of vengeance. What is vengeance? If a person says to another, "Lend me your spade," and he replies, "I will not lend it to you." The next day, the second party has to ask a similar favor from the first and says to him, "Lend me your spade," and the other replies, "I will not lend it to you, just as you did not lend me your spade when I asked it of you." This means taking revenge. He should rather give it to him cheerfully when he comes to ask for it, and must not repay him for his mistreatment....So too, whoever bears a grudge against a fellow Israelite violates a Negative *Mitzvah*. What is meant by "bearing a grudge?" A said to B, "Rent this house to me," or "Lend me this ox." B refused. After some time B comes to A to borrow or hire something. A replies, "Here it is; I am lending it to you; I am not like you; I will not treat you as you treated me." Whoever acts like this transgresses the command, "You shall not bear a grudge." One should blot the thing out of his mind and not cherish a grudge. For as long as he **cherishes a resentment** and keeps recalling it, he may come to avenge himself. For this reason, the *Torah* objects to bearing a grudge, that one may obliterate the wrong from his mind and remember it no more. This is the right way of behavior, whereby **civilization** and social intercourse are made possible.	**Spy**: An interesting use of the term in relation to Lashon Harah between neighbors. The word "spy" conjures up visions of war, espionage, battle and violence. With this one word, Maimonides teaches that there are those who see life as a war – they always like to "stir the pot." They can never get along with others and will use anything in their power to control others. **Leviticus 19:16**: By quoting *Torah*, Maimonides teaches that these laws are founded in the Covenant and form the foundation of our community. **Death**: Many people have died because of false rumors. In the history of the Jewish people one need only look to blood libel, where Jews were accused of using the blood of Christian children to bake Matzot, to understand how false rumors have destroyed many a community. This slander continues in the world to this present day. As Jews, we must be especially sensitive to this. **Ruins the world**: The direct opposite of "Tikun Olam," fixing the world. **The Truth**: The fascinating part of this sin is that tale bearing involves telling the truth, but shading it in such a way that it makes the victim look bad. It can also be telling the truth at a time when it will inflict maximum distress or damage on someone else. It is for this reason that Lashon Harah is considered equal to murder. At least with false rumors there is a possibility of proving it wrong. The truth stands. **Hear their talk**: Even listening to Lashon Harah is a sin because, by listening, you give the appearance of agreement to those around you. **In the wilderness**: this refers to the generation that left Egypt under Moses. They were condemned to wander in the wilderness for forty years until the death of their generation. Their sin? Twelve spies were sent out to bring back a report on the Promised Land. They came back and ten of the spies gave a report about a wonderful land which would be too hard to conquer. They told the truth! But in such a way as to make the truth unpalatable. There was a rebellion against Moses that was put down by force and punished by the forty years of wandering. **Sheer vanity**: The text suggests that before we become angry we reconsider and ask whether the issue is worth the anger. Someone refusing to lend you a shovel is just not that important in the broad scheme of things. **Cherishes a resentment**: There is a famous story about Clara Barton, the founder of the Red Cross, when reminded of some old slander, she professed that she had forgotten. When pressed, she responded, "I have forgotten about it, indeed, I distinctly remember forgetting about it." **Civilization**: Our text has a clear goal in mind. It wishes to teach us that we, as members of the community, must model the behavior that keeps the community united and healthy.

Appendix II
The Bill Emerson Good Samaritan Food Donation Act

In 1996, Congress enacted a piece of legislation commonly referred to as the "Bill Emerson Good Samaritan Food Donation Act." It appears in the Child Nutrition Act of 1996 as 42 U.S.C. 12672.

The fact is, you can't be sued if you donate leftover food
to a soup kitchen or a shelter. That's a fact.
(Danny Siegel, Mitzvahs, p. 24)

Bill Emerson Good Samaritan Food Donation Act

a Short title. This section may be cited as the "Bill Emerson Good Samaritan Food Donation Act."

b Definitions. As used in this section:

   1 Apparently fit grocery product. The term "apparently fit grocery product" means a grocery product that meets all quality and labeling standards imposed by Federal, State and local laws and regulations even though the product may not be readily marketable due to appearance, age, freshness, grade, size, surplus, or other conditions.

   2 Apparently wholesome food. The term "apparently wholesome food" means food that meets all quality and labeling standards imposed by Federal, State and local laws and regulation even though the food may not be readily marketable due to appearance, age, freshness, grade, size, surplus or other conditions.

   3 Donate. The term "donate" means to give without requiring anything of monetary value from the recipient, except that the term shall include giving by a nonprofit organization to another nonprofit organ-ization, notwithstanding that the donor organization has charged a nominal fee to the donating organization, if the ultimate recipient or user is not required to give anything of monetary value.

   4 Food. The term "food" means any raw, cooked, processed, or prepared edible substance, ice beverage, or ingredient used

or intended for use in whole or in part for human consumption.

5   Gleaner. The term "gleaner" means a person who harvests for free distribution to the needy, or for donation to a nonprofit organization for ultimate distribution to the needy, an agricultural crop that has been donated by the owner.

6   Grocery product. The term "grocery product" means a non-food grocery product, including a disposable paper or plastic product, household cleaning product, laundry detergent, cleaning product, or miscellaneous house-hold item.

7   Gross negligence. The term "gross negligence" means voluntary and conscious conduct (including failure to act) by a person who, at the time of the conduct, knew that the conduct was likely to be harmful to the health or well-being of another person.

8   Intentional misconduct. The term "intentional miscon-duct" means conduct by a person with knowledge (at the time of conduct) that the conduct is harmful to the health or well-being of another person.

9   Nonprofit organization. The term "nonprofit organ-ization" means an incorporated or unincorporated entity that –
   A   is operating for religious, charitable, or educational purposes; and
   B   does not provide net earning to, or operate in any other manner that inures to the benefit of, any officer, employee, or shareholder of the entity.

10 Person. The term "person" means an individual, corpora-tion, partnership, organization, association, or govern-mental entity, including a retail grocer, wholesaler, hotel, motel, manufacturer, restaurant, caterer, farmer, and nonprofit food distributor or hospital. In the case of a corporation, partnership, organization, association, or governmental entity, the term includes an officer, director, partner, deacon, trustee, council member, or other elected or

appointed individual responsible for the governance of the entity.

c Liability for damages for donated food and grocery products.
1 Liability of person or gleaner. A person or gleaner shall not be subject to civil or criminal liability arising from the nature, age, packaging or condition of apparently wholesome food or an apparently fit grocery product that the person or gleaner donates in good faith to a nonprofit organization for ultimate distribution to needy individuals.
2 Liability of nonprofit organization. A nonprofit organiz-ation shall not be subject to civil or criminal liability arising from the nature, age, packaging, or condition of apparently wholesome food or an apparently fit grocery product that the nonprofit organization received as a donation in good faith from a person or gleaner for ultimate distribution to needy individuals.
3 Exception. Paragraphs (1) and (2) shall not apply to an injury to or death of an ultimate user or recipient of the food or grocery product that results from an act or omission of the person, gleaner, or nonprofit organization, as applicable, constituting gross negli-gence or intentional misconduct.

d Collection or gleaning of donations. A person who allows the collection or gleaning of donations on property owned or occupied by the person by gleaners, or paid or unpaid representatives of a nonprofit organization, for ultimate distribution to needy individuals shall not be subject to civil or criminal liability that arises due to the injury or death of the gleaner or representative, except that this paragraph shall not apply to an injury or death that results from an act or omission of the person constituting gross negligence or intentional misconduct.

e Partial compliance. If some or all of the donated food and grocery products do not meet all quality and labeling standards imposed by Federal, State and local laws and regulations, the person or gleaner who donates the food and grocery products shall not be subject to civil or criminal liability in accordance with this section if the nonprofit organization that receives the donated food or grocery products –

1 Is informed by the donor of the distressed or defective condition of the donated food or grocery products.
2 Agrees to recondition the donated food or grocery products to comply with all the quality and labeling standards prior to distribution; and
3 Is knowledgeable of the standards to properly recondition the donated food or grocery product.

f Construction. This section shall not be construed to create any liability. Nothing in this section shall be construed to super-cede State or local health regulations.

(Nov. 16, 1990, P.L. 101-610, Title IV 402, 104 Stat. 3185. In addition, Oct 1, 1996, P.L. 1040210 transferred 42 U.S.C. 12672 as amended, from the National and Community Service Act of 1990 to the Child Nutrition Act of 1966; it was redesignated as section 22 of the Child Nutrition Act of 1966.)

Appendix III. Annotated Bibliography

Each family should have a *Tikun Olam* library for both adults and children. The following are the books I would buy first. Rather than list them in alphabetical order, I have listed them in the order I would buy them.

First Tier: For Children

Cone, Molly.. *Who Knows Ten? Children's Tales of the Ten Commandments.* Illustrated by Robin Brickman. New York: UAHC Press, 1998.

I believe this is the best story book ever written. Its stories are ethical, moving and powerful.

Jaffe, Nina. *In the Month of Kislev: A Story for Chanukah*, New York: Viking, 1992.

This is a children's story of high caliber. If you want to teach Tzedakah on Chanukah, this is the book. It is an easy read, an easier "read" out loud to children, and it teaches a great lesson about selfishness and Tzedakah.

For Families:

Grishaver, Joel. *40 Things You Can Do To Save the Jewish People*, Los Angeles: Alef Design Group; Los Angeles, 1993.

This is arguably the best book on Jewish continuity and education on the market today. You will learn more practical strategies for being Jewish from this book than from almost any other set of books you can name.

Klagsbrun, Francine, *Voices of Wisdom*, New York; Pantheon Books, 1980.

If you have never studied Jewish texts, or have dabbled infrequently and are intimidated by anything that looks like a text, this is a great starter book. It also has many texts that illustrate the lessons in this book.

For Parents and Grandparents:

Remen, Rachel Naomi, M.D. *My Grandfathers Blessings: Stories of Strength, Refuge, and Belonging,* New York: Riverhead Books, 2000

This is a most powerful book about individuals and families coping with illness and death. It is a book that has the ability to transform these experiences into sacred tasks.

2nd Tier:

Frankel, Ellen. *The Classic Tales: 4,000 Years of Jewish Lore*: New Jersey, Jason Aronson, 1993.

> *There are many stories in this collection which illustrate Mitzvot and Tikun Olam.*

Newman, Louis. *The Talmudic Anthology*, New York: Behrman House, 1945.

> *This book has many more texts than the Klagsbrun book, but no commentary.*

Schram, Peninnah. *Jewish Stories One Generation Tells Another*: New Jersey; Jason Aronson, 1989.

> *A book with many stories about Tikun Olam.*

Strassfeld, Michael, *The Jewish Holidays: A Guide & Commentary*, New York; Harper & Row, 1985.

> *I believe this is the best comprehensive book about the Jewish holy days on the market. It is a well thought out book with both basic information and incisive commentary on each Holy Day. Don't celebrate/observe a Holy Day without it.*

Thomas, Dr. William H. *Life Worth Living: How Someone You Love Can Still Enjoy Life in a Nursing Home*, MA; VanderWyk & Burnham, 1996.

> *This is a must read/have book for anyone who has a relative/friend/acquaintance who is in a nursing facility, nearing the age where they need to be in a nursing facility or contemplating placing a loved one in a nursing facility. It is a powerful statement about what is possible, and how living in a nursing facility does not have to be a "waiting to die" experience.*

Wiesel, Elie, *The Jews of Silence*, New York; Random House, 1978.
> *This book teaches about the mitzvot of "Do Not Stand Idly By," and "Redeeming Captives. It is powerful and troubling.*

In A Tier All Their Own:

Siegel, Danny. *Good People*, Pittsboro, North Carolina; Town House Press, 1995.

Gym Shoes & Irises, Book Two, Pittsboro, North Carolina, Town House Press, 1987.

Heroes & Miracle Workers, Pittsboro, North Carolina Town House Press, 1997. *Mitzvahs*, Pittsboro, North Carolina; Town House Press, 1992.

Mitzvahs, Pittsboro, North Carolina; Town House Press, 1992.

One cannot say enough about Danny – he is the mentor to the Tikun Olam movement. All his books are important, all teach the values.

Appendix IV. Annotated Videography

Absence of Malice: *Lashon Harah*, Refrain From Evil Language
Paul Newman teaches the Federal Government what can happen when they set out to destroy a person using evil language and slander. This is not a family film – but excellent for teens.

Aladdin: *Lechem L'reyvim*, Feeding the Hungry
Every Disney film has a message. Aladdin, near the beginning of the film, steals a loaf of bread – but shares it with beggar children. We learn he is not so bad after all. The rest of the film is just enjoyable.

Beauty & the Beast: *Hachnesat Orchim*, Hospitality and *Lehader Pnai Zaken*, Respect for Elders.
This is one of my "top ten" films. It is a story about redemption and atonement. The "beast" becomes a beast because he is unable to fulfill the Mitzvot of hospitality and respect for elders. He spends the rest of the film learning how. The entire film is his attempt to be a good host. Once he learns that a good host must love his guests, he is redeemed and turns back into a handsome prince.

Cocoon: *Lehader Pnai Zaken*, Respect for Elders.
The first scenes of Cocoon, where we see the nursing facility attached to the assisted residential homes is deeply emotional. It is hard to forget the scene where a man's definition of happiness is getting unmelted Hostess cupcakes. The entire film fights the stereotype of aging by portraying the elderly as human. It is a powerful film.

Groundhog Day: *Tikun Olam*.
Groundhog Day is the perfect Tikun Olam film. In it, a curmudgeon is forced to relive one day millions of times until he realizes that he must become a mensch. Give him at least a million days more to perfect his new persona and you have the essence of this film. Bill Murray must go through an entire day doing Mitzvot before he can get to the next day.

Joseph Shultz: *Al Ta'amod*, Do Not Stand Idly By.
> *Based upon a true story of the first days of World War Two, A German soldier refuses to execute innocent villagers. He is forced to bear their fate. It is very short (about 8 minutes long) and very powerful. This is not a film for children.*

Judgment at Nuremberg: *Al Ta'amod*, Do Not Stand Idly By
> *Perhaps a long version of Joseph Schultz. This movie is not about the trials of the "famous" Nazis. It is about the trials of German judges, those who upheld the Nazi laws. Were they correct to allow the Nazis to use their courts to pervert justice? The film examines this issue.*

Norma Rae: *Al Ta'amod*, Do Not Stand Idly By.
> *Based on a true story; a union organizer comes to a small Southern town to "unionize" a cotton mill.*

My Man Godfrey: *Tzedakah:*
> *It may be in black and white – but it's a great story especially if you like old movies. Instead of a handout a "forgotten man" is given a job – the rest is history as only William Powell and Carole Lombard can provide.*

The Fisher King: *Lashon Harah*, Refrain from Evil Language, *Tzedakah.*
> *This film tells us how evil language can kill. A shock-jock incites a person to murder. He cannot live with himself until by accident he meets one of the victims. There are excellent scenes about the meaning of Tzedakah – and what a person is allowed to do with it. This is not a family film – there is too much graphic language in it.*

The Shopping Bag Lady: *Tzedakah*
> *A short film about just that – a shopping bag lady.*

Weapons of the Spirit: *Al Ta'amod*, Do Not Stand Idly By
> *Did you know that in the midst of World War II, in France, over 5,000 Jews were hidden, in plain sight of the Nazis – and saved from the Holocaust? This film tells their story*

The people who put this book together...

Steven Bayar was ordained at the Reconstructionist Rabbinical College in 1981 and holds both a BA and MA in Biblical Studies and Medieval Jewish Philosophy from the University of Virginia. He served as Rabbi in Greenbelt, Maryland, and Chestnut Ridge, New York, before coming to Bnai Israel in Millburn in 1989.

He is the co-author, with Francine Hirschman, of *Teens & Trust: Building Bridges in Jewish Education* (TORAH AURA), *Rachel & Mischa*, with Ilene Strauss, (KAR-BEN), and *To Fix the World, with Naomi Eisenberger,* (KTAV) He is the author of *The Ziv Giraffe Mitzvah Hero Curriculum* for Steven Spielberg's Righteous Person's Foundation.

He has written over 50 curricula that are currently being used in over 1,000 educational programs throughout the United States and Canada . Some of his titles include: *Teaching Jewish Theology using Science Fiction & Fantasy*, and *Pirkei Avot: Ethics of the Ancestors,* in addition to more creative works such as curricula on *South Park, The Simpsons, Harry Potter* and *Disney.*

He is the proud father of Rahel & Tuvia, Meira and Merav and grandfather of Maayan.

Naomi Eisenberger is a founder and Executive Director of the GOOD PEOPLE FUND which began operation in 2008. Prior to that time she was the Managing Director of Danny Siegel's ZIV TZEDAKAH FUND and in that position learned first-hand about tzedakah, micro-philanthropy, and *tikkun olam,* repairing the world. She was also introduced to many *good people,* individuals who have dedicated themselves in numerous ways to making the world a better place.

Throughout her nearly two decades of tzedakah work, Naomi has learned that each of us has distinctive talents that can be used to change the world in ways both big and small. As a <u>parent</u> or <u>grandparent</u> we have a unique opportunity to guide and encourage our children and grandchildren to make them *good people* as well.

Her hope is that this book, based upon the highly successful Ziv Giraffe curriculum, will help in that quest.

Naomi and her husband Gerry have two children and five grandchildren.

Leora Aviv Wiener considers her greatest accomplishment to be the mother of two incredible boys, Matthew and Jesse, and has enjoyed three careers so far in her life. She holds two degrees in Linguistics, a BA from S.U.N.Y. at StoneyBrook and an MA. from the University of Chicago . She worked for the World Zionist Organization in editing and then in Market Research before she earned her BSN from Seton Hall University in nursing and is presently the nurse at the Millburn High School in Millburn, New Jersey.